12/24/11
To Dad,
Hope you enjoy
this inspirational
book, All my love,
Elaine

JOHN PAUL II
A Life of Grace

RENZO ALLEGRI

Translated by Marsha Daigle-Williamson, Ph.D.

SERVANT
BOOKS

PUBLISHED BY ST. ANTHONY MESSENGER PRESS
CINCINNATI, OHIO

Excerpts from *Love and Responsibility* by Karol Wojtyla, translated by H. T. Willetts. Translation ©1981 by Farrar, Straus & Giroux, Inc. and William Collins & Sons & Co., Ltd. Reprinted by permission of Farrar, Straus and Giroux, LLC.

Excerpt from *The Place Within: The Poetry of Pope John Paul II* by Pope John Paul II, ©1979, 1982 by Liberia Editrice Vaticana, Vatican City. Translation and notes ©1979, 1982 by Jerzy Peteriewicz. Used by permission of Random House, Inc.

Excerpt from *Poland* by James Michener ©1983 by James A. Michener. Used by permission of Random House, Inc.

Excerpt from *Pilgrim to Poland* by John Paul II, compiled by the Daughters of St. Paul (Pauline Books & Media, 1979). Used by permission.

Excerpts from *Witness to Hope* by George Weigel ©1999 by George Weigel. Reprinted by permission of Harper Collins Publishers, Inc.

Excerpts from *His Holiness* by Carl Bernstein and Marco Politi, ©1996 by Carl Bernstein and Marco Politi. Used by permission of Doubleday, a division of Random House, Inc.

Excerpts from *Gift and Mystery* by Pope John Paul II, ©1996 by Libreria Editrice Vaticana. Used by permission of Doubleday, a division of Random House, Inc.

Scripture quotation on page 67 is taken from the *New Revised Standard Version Bible*, copyright ©1989 by the Division of Christian Education of the National Council of the Churches of Christ in the U.S.A., and used by permission. All rights reserved.

Cover design by Candle Light Studios
Book design by Phillips Robinette, O.F.M.

Library of Congress Cataloging-in-Publication Data

Allegri, Renzo.
    John Paul II : a life of grace / Renzo Allegri ; translated by Marsha Daigle-Williamson.
        p. cm.
    Includes bibliographical references.
    ISBN 0-86716-657-6 (alk. paper)
    1. John Paul II, Pope, 1920- 2. Popes—Biography. I. Title.
    BX1378.5.A37 2005
    282'.092—dc22

                                2004026080

ISBN 0-86716-657-6
Copyright ©2005 by Renzo Allegri. All rights reserved.

Published by Servant Books, an imprint of St. Anthony Messenger Press,
28 W. Liberty St., Cincinnati, OH 45202
www.AmericanCatholic.org
Printed in the United States of America.

05 06 07 08 09 10 9 8 7 6 5 4 3 2 1

Table of Contents

A Record-Setting Pope

O N MARCH 17, 2004, John Paul II became the second longest reigning pope in the Church's history. On that date he surpassed Leo XIII, the pope of *Rerum Novarum* fame, having reigned twenty-five years, five months and one day. Excluding Peter, whose dates as pope are uncertain, Pius IX reigned the longest of the 264 pontiffs—almost thirty-two years.

John Paul II has other records to his name. He is the first Polish pope, the first pope to come from a communist country, the first Slavic pope, the first pope who was an actor, the first pope to pray in a synagogue, the first pope to enter a mosque and the first to concelebrate Mass with Orthodox priests. He is also the first pope to acknowledge errors committed during the course of Church history, reevaluating people such as Galileo Galilei, Savonarola, Martin Luther and Giordano Bruno, whom his predecessors had condemned.

TWENTY-FIVE YEARS

These unique characteristics, together with many more important spiritual qualities, were highlighted on October 16, 2003, when John Paul II celebrated a quarter century as pope. The ceremonies marking this anniversary began May 8, 2003, with a two-day academic congress at the Lateran University entitled "John Paul II, Twenty-Five Years of Papacy: The Church at the Service of Humanity." On Sunday, May 11, opening celebrations began in Kraków through a joint collaboration of the Italian and Polish governments. The Italian government enlisted the Italian Institute for Cultural Relations to develop exhibits inspired by Karol Wojtyla's quote, "Italy is my second home." In fact, during his twenty-five years as pope, John Paul II has become the most visible "ambassador" for the Italian language in the world.

The Vatican, in collaboration with Poland, issued a stamp depicting the pope and his coat-of-arms. There was also a series of stamps with twenty-five different pictures of the pope and a limited edition of eight different coins.

John Paul II initiated the major festivities on October 7 with a pilgrimage to the Shrine of Our Lady of the Rosary at Pompeii. There he declared the end of the "Year of the Rosary," proclaimed in 2002, and entrusted the celebration of his twenty-five years of papacy to the protection of Mary.

Cardinal Joseph Ratzinger, prefect for the Congregation of the Doctrine of Faith and dean of the College of Cardinals, had invited all of the cardinals to Rome. On the morning of October 16, the anniversary of John Paul II's election, they participated in a solemn Mass in St. Peter's Square, where an enormous crowd had gathered. On October 17 and 18 the cardinals attended a conference at which five addresses were given, concluding with a "message to the Holy Father."

On the morning of October 19 the pope presided over the solemn beatification of Mother Teresa of Calcutta. As a sign of his admiration for the diminutive nun, he intentionally chose to have this ceremony added to the celebration schedule. On October 21 the celebrations concluded with the Pope's naming of thirty new cardinals.

HISTORY WILL REMEMBER

Radio, television, newspapers, magazines—every segment of Italian and foreign media covered the event. Commentators noted that this pope was already legendary, and with good cause. He has had a positive influence on world history as few individuals have. He will be included in encyclopedias but not only as a religious figure. In fact, he is famous for his literary activity—as a poet, a dramatist and a philosopher—and has contributed substantial works in all these disciplines. But for Catholics he is, above all, a shining and extraordinary example of spirituality, a true saint whose long life, beset by trials, has been punctuated by numerous mysterious events, powerful charisms and authentic miracles.

John Paul II has played a significant role in the historical, social and religious events at the end of the twentieth century. These events brought revolutionary changes in the human community and meant that the third Christian millennium would begin, despite a multitude of uncertainties and difficulties, in a spiritual atmosphere of considerable optimism.

Pope John Paul II especially contributed to communism's downfall in a significant way. Historians admit that atheistic communism was a political and ideological experiment that was harmful to humanity. According to the estimate of historians, twentieth-century communism caused between 120 million and 150 million deaths of people whose faith or ideology was deemed unacceptable.

Many intellectuals and politicians combated this ideology, and John Paul II was a front-runner among them. However, simultaneously and with the same vigor, he also fought the dangers of capitalism, consumerism, hedonism, secularism, atheism, racism, egoism, fundamentalism, apathy, fear, hate and war. In short, he opposed anything that injures human beings and their dignity as distinct and unique individuals.

He is the "pilgrim pope" *par excellence,* having visited almost the entire Catholic world. He has completed 246 apostolic trips—144 in Italy and 102 internationally, covering 130 countries and 615 different cities. He has traveled about 776,250 miles to preach the gospel, a distance equivalent to circling the globe thirty-nine times and almost three times the distance between the earth and the moon. He has given 2,499 speeches.

In 1986 he visited the Synagogue of Rome. In 1993 he established the first official diplomatic relations between Israel and the Holy See. His trips to countries in the East—to Sarajevo, Beirut, Jerusalem and Sinai; his asking forgiveness on behalf of the Church; his World Youth Days; and his meetings in Rome during the Great Jubilee of 2000 are all milestones. He has published fourteen encyclicals, has given thousands of speeches, has canonized five hundred saints and declared fifteen hundred people blessed.

He is one of the few popes in history to have survived an assassination attempt. In May 13, 1981, when Alì Agca shot him in the abdomen at close range, the strong, athletic, indefatigable pope, whom all the world admired, became a suffering pope. Illnesses, accidents, hospitalizations and surgeries have continued in succession, causing him much pain.

During the celebrations of his twenty-five years as pope, the inexorable television cameras did not lie. There he was for all the world to see, burdened by sorrow, afflicted by illnesses. He is truly, as someone has written, "a living crucified one." But these difficulties have not squelched his passionate spiritual commitment. He sees his mission as a mission to all people: Protestants, Orthodox, Jews, Muslims and atheists.

"*HABEMUS PAPAM*"

This fantastic adventure began on October 16, 1978. At 7:20 P.M. Karol Wojtyla, the new pontiff of the Catholic Church, appeared on the central balcony of St. Peter's Basilica. "Praised be Jesus Christ," he said in a decisive and steady voice. His opening remarks to the world outlined the theme of his papacy.

One hour earlier, at 6:18 P.M., the traditional white smoke had risen from the smokestack of the Sistine Chapel, announcing that the 111 cardinals of the Catholic Church, who had been meeting in conclave for two days, had elected a new pope. The majority of Italians were watching their televisions. I was watching a gigantic monitor in the editorial room of the newspaper I was working for. My colleagues and I were having an animated discussion about the cardinals who might have been chosen.

At 6:43 the television cameras focused on the group of ecclesiastics on the central balcony who would reveal the name of the elected pope. The protodeacon, Cardinal Pericle Felici, announced, "*Habemus papam.* We have a pope. His Most Reverend Eminence Monsignor Karol, Cardinal of the Holy Roman Church, Wojtyla, who has taken the name John Paul II."

In my editing room there was stunned silence. This was a name that was entirely unknown. Consulting the list of cardinals published in the newspapers, we learned that Karol Wojtyla was Polish, the archbishop of Kraków. There were no biographical notes on him, as he was not part of the group of papal possibilities discussed by the mass media.

One of my colleagues rushed to the phone, dialed directory assistance for international numbers and asked to speak to the archdiocesan office in Kraków. After a few minutes she got through. The newswoman said in English that an extraordinary event had happened in Rome, but no one on the other end understood English. Then she said it in French—nothing. She tried in Italian, which they understood a little.

There was a moment of silence at the other end of the line, then a request for clarification. After that someone shouted. Very excited voices were heard in the background, but then the connection was lost. I believe that it was my colleague who first announced to Kraków that their cardinal had become pope.

Radio and television interrupted their normal programming and set up links to St. Peter's Square, which was quickly filling with Romans. One hour after the white smoke had dissipated, the windows of the balcony opened and the newly elected pope appeared. The normal ritual called for him to give an apostolic blessing in Latin but not to speak. However, Wojtyla perceived the bafflement and the tension among the crowd because he was a foreigner, and he decided to deal immediately with that concern. He approached the microphone.

"Praised be Jesus Christ," he said in a firm and graceful voice. It was the voice of a CEO, of a head of state, of someone used to speaking before crowds. He continued:

> Dearest brothers and sisters, we are all still grieving the death of our most beloved John Paul I. And now the most eminent cardinals have named a new Bishop of Rome. They have called him from a distant country…distant, but nevertheless near through the communion of faith and of Christian tradition.[1]

We could hear the foreign accent, but his pronunciation was clear. The words "called from a distant country" lifted the veil to betray some emotion, and the Roman people responded with heartfelt applause. The pope continued:

I was afraid in accepting this position, but I have done it in the spirit of obedience to Our Lord Jesus Christ and in total trust toward his Mother, Our Lady. I don't know if I can explain myself well in your...in our Italian language.[2]

His self-correction evoked enormous applause, interspersed with the shout, "Long live the pope!" John Paul II had conquered the Romans, as well as the Italians who were following the speech on television. Even warmer applause followed his next sentence: "If I make a mistake, please correct me."

Applause interrupted the pope as he continued:

And so I present myself to all of you, to profess our common faith, our hope, and our trust in the Mother of Christ and in the Church, and to begin a new page in history and in the Church, with God's help and the help of the people.[3]

"Leave for Rome immediately," my editor-in-chief said. A similar order certainly came from other newspaper editors in Italy and abroad. Hearing about this vigorous, athletic man with the lean, tan face, they understood that a pontiff had come to the throne of Peter who was very different from those in the past. He was a new pope with an unusual style and an unusual personality.

FACTS AND FAITH

Since Karol Wojtyla's election twenty-six years ago, innumerable biographies, books, commentaries, feature stories and essays have been written about him and the things he has done. John Paul II has lived under the relentless eye of the camera and has sat in front of media microphones willingly,

calmly and patiently. All aspects of his life have been ana-
lyzed—including his acting when he was young and his work
as a poet and a playwright, which he continued even as a cardinal. People have relished this pontiff who swims in pools,
skis in the Apennines and hikes through the Alpine forests.

For someone to think about writing something new about
John Paul II seems ludicrous—unless one is willing to examine the dimension of his life that goes beyond time and con-
tingency into the invisible world. Here I recount events and
coincidences that make sense only if one accepts mystery. Even
believers can fear being called "visionaries" if they acknowledge the mysterious events I explore in this book. But this
approach is in perfect harmony with the faith, as it links the
story of time to the supernatural—to God and to eternity.

CHAPTER ONE

"The Bishop Dressed in White" ✝

THERE ARE NUMEROUS SIGNS that God himself chose and prepared John Paul II for his mission in the contemporary world. The choice occurred even before his birth. The pope affirmed this when he recognized himself in the third secret of Fatima, which was revealed by Our Lady to three young Portuguese children in 1917, three years before Wojtyla was born.

In May 2000 John Paul II went to Fatima for the beatification of Jacinta and Francisco, the two shepherd visionaries who died in their youth. The Great Jubilee was taking place in Rome. The eighty-year-old John Paul II was burdened by many serious obligations; moreover, he was not in good health. He could have celebrated the beatification ceremony in Rome, as he had done for so many others. Instead he wanted to celebrate the occasion at Fatima, no matter what the cost.

The reason for his decision became known at the end of the solemn religious rite. Cardinal Angelo Sodano, Secretary of State at the Vatican, speaking before the enormous crowd gathered in the square and before millions of television viewers, announced that John Paul II had decided to finally reveal the third part of the famous secret of Fatima. He added that the pope recognized himself in that part of the secret. This secret had been spoken about since 1917. The three visionaries—Lucia, Francisco and Jacinta—referred to a secret Our Lady had given them but said nothing else about it, even under intense pressure from the clergy and civil authorities. Only after many years did Lucia obtain permission from Our Lady to reveal the first two parts of the secret, and in 1944 she revealed the third part to Pope Pius XII. She left the occasion of making it public to his discretion and that of his successors.

As we learned in May 2000, the third part of the secret was closely linked to John Paul II and his papacy. The pope himself has said it and has had his closest associates repeat it. This information has become key for interpreting the whole life of the pope. If he is the protagonist in a story that the Blessed Virgin spoke about in 1917, then every moment of his life needs to be interpreted according to that story. It is therefore necessary to understand the details of what happened at Fatima.

THE APPARITIONS

Our Lady first appeared to three children in Cova da Iria on the outskirts of Fatima on May 13, 1917. The three children were Lucia dos Santo, age ten; Francisco Marto, age eight; and Jacinta, Francisco's sister, age six. Our Lady told them she wanted to meet them again in that location on the thirteenth day of every month until October. And so the apparitions continued, along with different events that typically accompany such supernatural appearances. People began to gather at Cova da Iria. Almost a hundred thousand people would witness the great and final event on October 13.

The apparitions at Fatima, which received ecclesiastical approval in 1930, are some of the most well-known apparitions. This is particularly true because of the famous third secret of Fatima. Thousands of articles and hundreds of books have been written about that secret. There have been rumors of every kind concerning it, right up until the appointed time for the complete revelation by John Paul II in May 2000.

Our Lady gave the secret to the three children on July 13, 1917, during her third appearance at Fatima. Cova da Iria resembled a large village festival on that day, with more than four thousand people gathered from all over. Around noon the children arrived and stood near the small holmoak tree above which they said Our Lady would appear. The crowd thronged around them. Everyone wanted to be as close as possible to witness the apparition.

Lucia knelt and began reciting the rosary. The young girl's voice filled the valley. The crowd listened in absolute silence to the first part of the "Hail Mary" and responded in unison.

Finishing the rosary, Lucia stood to her feet. "There, I see the lamp. Our Lady is coming," she cried. As in preceding apparitions, at that moment the sun became clouded over and a light breeze began to blow. The crowd was silent.

Lucia later recounted what Our Lady said:

> I want you to come here on the thirteenth of next month, to continue to pray the rosary every day in honor of Our Lady of the Rosary, in order to obtain peace for the world and the end of the war, because only she can help you.[1]

"I would like to ask you to tell us who you are, and to work a miracle so that everybody will believe that you are appearing to us," said Lucia. The request came from the anxiety that Lucia had been experiencing for some time that this beautiful Lady might be a demonic illusion.

Our Lady reassured the young girl, "Continue to come here every month. In October, I will tell you who I am and what I want, and I will perform a miracle for all to see and believe." She paused and continued:

> Sacrifice yourselves for sinners, and say many times, especially whenever you make some sacrifice: "O Jesus, it is for love of you, for the conversion of sinners, and in reparation for the sins committed against the Immaculate Heart of Mary." [2]

THE MESSAGE

The Blessed Virgin opened her hands, as she had done during the two earlier appearances. The following is Lucia's account, from her memoirs, of what happened then:

> Our Lady showed us a great sea of fire which seemed to be under the earth. Plunged in this fire were demons and souls in human form, like transparent burning embers, all blackened or burnished bronze, floating about in the conflagration, now raised into the air by the flames that issued from within themselves together with great clouds of smoke, now falling back on every side like sparks in huge fires, without weight or equilibrium, and amid shrieks and groans of pain and despair, which horrified us and made us tremble with fear. The demons could be distinguished by their terrifying and repellent likeness to frightful and unknown animals, black and transparent like burning coals. This vision lasted but an instant. How can we ever be grateful enough to our kind heavenly Mother, who had already prepared us by promising, in the first Apparition, to take us to heaven. Otherwise, I think we would have died of fear and terror.
> We then looked up at Our Lady, who said to us so kindly and so sadly:
> "You have seen hell where the souls of poor sinners go. To save them, God wishes to establish in the world devotion to my Immaculate Heart. If what I say to you is done, many souls will be saved and there will be peace. The war is going to end; but if people do not cease offending God, a worse one will break out during the Pontificate of Pius XI. When you see a night illumined by

an unknown light, know that this is the great sign given you by God that he is about to punish the world for its crimes, by means of war, famine, and persecutions of the Church and of the Holy Father.

"To prevent this, I shall come to ask for the consecration of Russia to my Immaculate Heart, and the Communion of reparation on the First Saturdays. If my requests are heeded, Russia will be converted, and there will be peace; if not, she will spread her errors throughout the world, causing wars and persecutions of the Church. The good will be martyred; the Holy Father will have much to suffer; various nations will be annihilated. In the end, my Immaculate Heart will triumph. The Holy Father will consecrate Russia to me, and she will be converted, and a period of peace will be granted to the world…. In Portugal, the dogma of the faith will always be preserved…." [3]

Lucia's manuscript breaks off at this point. The ellipses indicate that she is leaving out the rest of what Our Lady said. It has to do with what is called "the third part" of the secret of Fatima. This part Our Lady told Lucia not to share. Only years later did people find out what this secret was, or at least part of this secret.

Lucia then asked the Blessed Virgin, "Is there anything more that you want of me?"

"No, I do not want anything more of you today." Then, as before, Our Lady rose up in an eastward direction and disappeared into the immensity of the sky.

Eyewitness testimony recounts that at that very moment a loud clap of thunder was heard. Near the small holmoak tree was a wire on which two lanterns hung, forming a kind of ark. The lanterns began to oscillate as if there were an earthquake. Many spectators stated that during the apparition there was a small luminous cloud over the holmoak tree, and they heard a hum coming from the cloud in response to Lucia's question, like the sound from a hornets' nest.

At the end of the apparition people approached the three children and asked them questions. When they asked Lucia what Mary said, Lucia replied that the Virgin told them many things. They asked why Lucia had let out a cry of fear, but the child said she couldn't tell; it was a secret that was good for some but bad for others. When they pressed her to learn when she could divulge the secret, Lucia would only say that she didn't know.

THE SECRET

Francisco died in 1919 at the age of eleven; Jacinta died the following year at the age of ten. Neither revealed anything about the secret, even on their deathbeds. Lucia entered the convent, and only in 1927 did she obtain permission from the Blessed Virgin to reveal the first two parts of the secret. Our Lady appeared to her as she was praying in the chapel for novitiates.

Lucia spoke with her confessor, who told her to write everything down, but it seems that he returned those pages to her without even reading them. Lucia also spoke with two Jesuits, with the provincial superior of the Dorothean Order and with the bishop of Leiria. But no one treated what she had to say as important.

In the first two parts of the secret the Blessed Virgin focused the children's attention—and through them everyone else's attention—on the fundamental truths of the faith: the existence of God and eternal life after death, with heaven as a reward for doing good and hell for those who rebel against God. These truths the Church already held as traditional doctrines, but they had been neglected in her teaching and forgotten by many. Evidently, Our Lady wanted the people of God to reflect on these truths, especially in the near future, when they would be neglected more and even doubted. Yet she asked the three children not to reveal what she had told them for the time being.

To better understand the context of this message, we should recall how Catholic doctrine interprets life. Man and woman were given a unique gift when they were created: free will. Human beings are the only creatures gifted with absolute moral freedom. Not even angels are free the way humans are. In every moment of life people may choose to be with God or to set themselves against God.

From the very beginning the man and the woman were surrounded by evil spirits. In Revelation 12 John speaks of a time when there was a great battle in heaven. Some of the angels rebelled against God. They fought against the faithful angels but were defeated and thrown out of heaven. They became the forces of evil, the enemies of God. Since they were not able to harm God or the faithful angels, they turned their attention to the man and the woman. The enemies tried to incite them to rebel against their creator.

Their efforts succeeded with Adam. Listening to suggestions from Satan, Adam broke his union with God both for himself and for his descendants. But God, in His infinite goodness, wanted to repair the breach by sending his own Son, Jesus, the new Adam, who sacrificed himself to redeem the world, restoring to men and women their dignity as sons and daughters of God.

But even after redemption people remain weak and vulnerable, their minds like clouded lenses. Humanity's enemies know that and profit from it. The battle for salvation is difficult, but Jesus, Our Lady, the angels and the saints never stop helping, even with extraordinary interventions like apparitions. Our Lady especially acts this way, because as a mother she knows better than anyone else the difficulties of her children.

At Fatima Our Lady came to bring extraordinary help. She wanted to draw people's attention to the worst danger, the eternal enemy, Satan, a murderer from the beginning, the one who inspires all evil and is determined to drag as many people as possible into eternal perdition. She offered herself as a weapon for salvation, a sure help against that enemy. She indicated that, through the will of God, her "Immaculate Heart" is an inexhaustible fount of energy needed to win the last battle. That is the message of the first two parts of the secret of Fatima.

THE THIRD PART

In 1944 Our Lady told Lucia she could reveal the third part of the secret but only to the pope. Lucia was in Tuy, Spain. She wrote out the third part, signed it and dated it January 3, 1944. She included a letter to the pope, advising him of Our Lady's wish that this third secret not be made public before 1960. After that the pope had discretion about when to reveal it. Lucia sealed the envelope, addressed it to Pope Pius XII and sent it inside a letter to her own bishop to facilitate its arrival at the Vatican.

Pius XII observed the guidelines set forth by Lucia. In 1958 John XXIII became pope. The following year he read through Lucia's letter but decided not to reveal the secret. The successive popes, Paul VI, John Paul I and John Paul II, did the same.

The fact that any pope after 1960 could reveal what Our Lady had told the children but had not done so increased people's curiosity. Rumors, conjectures and speculations began to circulate. People talked about the destruction of the world and nuclear war. Some said that John XXIII had sent the content of the secret to world leaders, who then disseminated apocalyptic predictions that it contained.

In 1981 the assassination attempt against John Paul II occurred. The following year the pope visited Fatima, where he said his life had been saved by the intervention of Our Lady. The end of the 1980s saw the collapse of communism, foreseen in the second part of the secret. These events all fueled speculation about the third part of the secret.

When it was announced in 2000 that the pope would reveal the third part of the secret, ecclesiastical authorities sought to temper people's expectations by proceeding in stages. They began by focusing attention on how the language of visions should be interpreted. After the ceremony for the beatification of Francisco and Jacinta on May 13, 2000, in Fatima, Cardinal Sodano spoke briefly, inviting people to calm reflection and indicating the guidelines people should use in thinking about this vision:

> On this solemn occasion of his visit to Fatima, His Holiness has directed me to make an announcement to you. As you know, the purpose of his visit to Fatima has been to beatify the two "little shepherds." Nevertheless he also wishes his pilgrimage to be a renewed gesture of gratitude to Our Lady for her protection during these years of his papacy. This protection seems also to be linked to the so-called third part of the "secret" of Fatima.
>
> That text contains a prophetic vision similar to those found in Sacred Scripture, which do not describe with photographic clarity the details of future events, but rather synthesize and condense against a unified background events spread out over time in a succession and a duration which are not specified. As a result, the text must be interpreted in a symbolic key.[4]

Sodano was throwing water on the fire, but he explicitly assented to the fact that the secret had to do with the 1981 attempt on the pope's life. The pope had said on numerous occasions that he believed Our Lady had saved his life at that time. And Sodano affirmed that this "protection seems also to be linked to the so-called third part of the 'secret' of Fatima."

"Seems," Sodano had said. But that *seems,* pronounced on such an occasion before millions of faithful, took on the weight of almost certainty. Otherwise the Church, in her infinite wisdom and through the wishes of the pope himself, would not have exposed herself in that way.

The text of the secret became a public document on June 26, 2000, during a press conference at the Vatican. Cardinal Joseph Ratzinger, prefect for the Congregation for the Doctrine of the Faith, was present. The text Lucia had written in 1944 was very brief—one page in all:

> I write in obedience to you, my God, who command me to do so through his Excellency the Bishop of Leiria and through your Most Holy Mother and mine.
>
> After the two parts which I have already explained, at the left of Our Lady and a little above, we saw an Angel with a flaming sword in his left hand; flashing, it gave out flames that looked as though they would set the world on fire; but they died out in contact with the splendour that Our Lady radiated towards him from her right hand: pointing to the earth with his right hand, the Angel cried out in a loud voice: "Penance, Penance, Penance!" And we saw in an immense light that is God: 'something similar to how people appear in a mirror when they pass in front of it,' a Bishop dressed in White. We had the impression that it was the Holy Father. Other Bishops, Priests, men and women Religious going up a steep mountain, at the top of which there was a big Cross of rough-hewn trunks as of a cork-tree with the bark; before reaching there the Holy Father passed through a big city half in ruins and half trembling with halting step, afflicted with pain and sorrow, he prayed for the souls of the corpses he met on his way; having reached the top of the mountain, on his knees at the foot of the big Cross he was killed by a group of soldiers who fired bullets and arrows at him, and in the same way there died one after another the other Bishops, Priests, men and women Religious, and various lay people of different ranks and positions. Beneath the two arms of the Cross there were two Angels each with a crystal aspersorium in his hand, in which they gathered up

the blood of the Martyrs and with it sprinkled the souls that were making their way to God.

—Tuy, January 3, 1944[5]

Many were disappointed at the reading of this page. They were expecting disconcerting revelations: predictions of war, disaster, catastrophes and nuclear destruction. Some believed that the Holy See had not revealed the whole text.

The Secret and John Paul II

We will not get into the merits of different assessments and appraisals. The incontrovertible issue that is of interest to this book is the fact that this part of the secret concerned John Paul II. That was the pope's conviction, and he made it known publicly. It was a conviction arising from the words of the secret but also certainly from the conversations the pope had with Sister Lucia.

Cardinal Sodano said in his Fatima speech on May 13, 2000:

> According to the interpretation of the "little shepherds," which was also confirmed recently by Sister Lucia, "the Bishop clothed in white" who prays for all the faithful is the Pope. As he makes his way with great difficulty towards the Cross amid the corpses of those who were martyred (Bishops, priests, men and women Religious and many lay people), he too falls to the ground, apparently dead, under a hail of gunfire.
>
> After the assassination attempt of 13 May 1981, it appeared evident that it was "a mother's hand that guided the bullet's path," enabling "the Pope in his throes" to halt "at the threshold of death" (Pope John Paul II, *Meditation from the Policlinico Gemelli to the Italian Bishops, Insegnamenti*, XVII, 1 [1994], 1061).
>
> On the occasion of a visit to Rome by the then Bishop of Leiria-Fatima, the Pope decided to give him the bullet which had remained in the jeep after the assassination attempt, so that it might be kept in the shrine. By the Bishop's decision, the bullet was later set in the crown of the statue of Our Lady of Fatima.[6]

It should be noted that Cardinal Sodano wanted to recount the facts using the pontiff's own words, and those are the phrases in quotation marks. He wanted to point out that the pope had no doubts that the "Bishop dressed in white," seen by the children in the vision, was none other than himself, John Paul II. The pope was part of a story told three years before he was born.

Cardinal Ratzinger, in the presentation of the secret on June 26 at the Vatican, did all he could to limit and, in a sense, minimize the prophetic discourse's tie to John Paul II. He wanted the text to have a long introduction focusing on how the faithful should interpret the visions. He tried to give the text a general sense, to apply it to all the pontiffs of the twentieth century. At the same time he had to respect the pope's conviction, which John Paul has expressed often, that in these words there was an explicit reference to John Paul II. The cardinal posed rhetorical questions:

> In the *Via Crucis* [Way of the Cross] of an entire century, the figure of the Pope has a special role. In his arduous ascent of the mountain we can undoubtedly see a convergence of different Popes. Beginning from Pius X up to the present Pope, they all shared the sufferings of the century and strove to go forward through all the anguish along the path which leads to the Cross. In the vision, the Pope too is killed along with the martyrs. When, after the attempted assassination on 13 May 1981, the Holy Father had the text of the third part of the "secret" brought to him, was it not inevitable that he should see in it his own fate? He had been very close to death, and he himself explained his survival in the following words: "…it was a mother's hand that guided the bullet's path and in his throes the Pope halted at the threshold of death" (13 May 1994). That here "a mother's hand" had deflected the fateful bullet only shows once more that there is no immutable destiny, that faith and prayer are forces which can influence history and that in the end prayer is more powerful than bullets and faith more powerful than armies.[7]

These interesting observations from Cardinal Ratzinger merit reflection. They confirm the fact that John Paul II recognized himself in a prophecy from the Blessed Virgin on July 13, 1917, three years before his birth. The pope has acknowledged that when Our Lady appeared at Fatima, gave the children her message and confided to them her concerns about the future of humanity, she had Karol Wojtyla in mind. She knew about his life, she knew what he would do, and she chose him as a collaborator for a mission to help save the world.

DEFEATING THE ENEMY

However, another personality is on the scene: Satan. The existence of this being is a fundamental truth of Christian doctrine. Our Lady wants to help save the world, while her bitter enemy does all he can to get people to refuse salvation. At Fatima, at Lourdes and in every contact the Blessed Virgin has with people, she encourages us to flee the insidious designs of Satan, whose goal is the eternal perdition of souls.

The first part of the secret of Fatima concerns the existence of hell and the perdition of rebellious souls. The second part concerns the disasters that Satan would sow in the world and how to avoid those disasters. Because so many people have not availed themselves of the helps proposed by the Blessed Virgin, the third part revolves around the works of Satan: a city in ruins, corpses, persecutions, killings and the pope, with trembling and halting steps, moving toward the mountain, where he is killed.

The scenario is unmistakable. Satan is the author of the destruction, the wars and the hate that devastate the world because he is the "prince of this world," a "murderer from the beginning." In the plan of salvation the Blessed Virgin proposes herself as the "sure path" to overcome Satan's snares.

It was Karol Wojtyla who gave credence to the Blessed Virgin's request for the consecration of Russia to the Immaculate Heart of Mary. This he did on March 25, 1984. Five years later the Berlin Wall fell, communist regimes were floundering, Gorbachev went to Rome to visit John Paul II's Vatican, and religious freedom was restored in Russia. The Blessed Virgin's plan is, at least in part, already accomplished, but at the price of many victims and much suffering.

Satan did what he could to prevent the fulfillment of this plan of salvation. He set into motion a thousand traps to destroy Wojtyla, even physically. If we look at the history of this man's life, it is hard to believe how many dangers, snares, accidents and mysterious circumstances he has had to overcome to achieve the destiny that was predicted by the Blessed Virgin at Fatima. One could call all these things coincidences, of course. But they are so unique, so related, so numerous and so haunting that it seems very unlikely they are merely chance occurrences.

CHAPTER TWO

Origins

MANY DIFFICULTIES STOOD IN the way of Karol Wojtyla's birth. It was as though obscure, mysterious forces set themselves against the Wojtyla family, especially against the mother of the future pope. The woman gave birth to this son after sixteen years of marriage, against the advice of doctors who wanted her to abort the child.

These are difficulties that can happen in any family, someone could say. That is true, but the thought immediately arises that the adversity in this case was put into place by the enemy, who knew about the apparitions at Fatima and sought to prevent the mission from being fulfilled.

The mother of the future John Paul II was Emilia Kaczorowska, the daughter of a Lithuanian upholsterer. She was born in Silesia on March 26, 1884, one of nine siblings. The family moved to Kraków when Emilia was still very young.

Documents about Emilia's life are very rare, but we do know that she was afflicted by sorrows and misfortunes. In a very few years she lost four siblings as well as her mother. She attended a school run by the Sisters of Mercy but was only able to attend elementary school. She became a seamstress and a laundress to help support the family, and she helped raise her younger siblings. She was frail and sickly.

The father of the future pope was Karol Wojtyla. He was born August 18, 1879, in Linik, the son of a tailor. He attended elementary school and three years of high school. He received a good education, better than average for young people at that time, and learned his father's trade.

In 1900 the senior Wojtyla was called up to the Austrian army. He stayed on after his term of duty ended, attaining the rank of noncommissioned officer. His military career allowed him to leave behind the meager existence of village life and to continue his studies, which he very much enjoyed. During World War I his heroic actions were publicly rewarded with the Iron Cross of Merit.

Karol and Emilia became acquainted at the Catholic Church in Kraków. Emilia immediately fell in love with the young soldier. According to a report from the Austrian army, Karol was considered by his superiors to be "honest, loyal, serious, educated, humble, upright, responsible, generous, and tireless." These were qualities Emilia admired.

Photographs show an attractive couple. Maria Janina Kaczorowa, a neighbor of the family who was still alive when the younger Wojtyla was elected pope, described the pontiff's parents:

> He was tall, with very straight shoulders, and he had a graceful stride. His high boots and the three shiny stars of the noncommissioned officer on his collar gave him an elegant appeal. He was very admired by young women.

Emilia Kaczorowska was the most beautiful, elegant young woman in Wadowice. She was slender and had deep-set dark eyes and a disarming smile. Her personality was joyful and always peaceful. She made her own clothes and dressed modestly, but in a distinctively feminine way. She had long hair, which she wore piled on top of her head, which was the fashion at that time.[1]

Karol and Emilia were married on February 10, 1904, in Kraków, in the church of St. Peter and St. Paul, which was the city's church for the military. They lived in Kraków for a while and then moved to Wadowice.

THE POPE'S SIBLINGS

On August 26, 1906, Emilia gave birth to a baby boy they named Edmund. From the time of this delivery, Emilia's delicate health worsened. The doctors told her to be content with her one child because future pregnancies would have serious health consequences.

The family led a peaceful life. Karol's salary was not large, but it sufficed. Emilia managed the books with great thrift and prudence. She also worked as a seamstress to contribute to the family budget. She liked to dress her baby well, so she would model the clothes she made for him after those in the most fashionable shops in Kraków.

Edmund was a healthy, lively and intelligent boy. His family nickname was Mundek. When he started going to school, he studied hard and did well. Emilia decided that her son should attend college and become an important person. She was proud of him.

In 1914 Emilia became pregnant again. Her pregnancy was difficult this time, and the delivery was complicated. The baby girl, Olga, lived only a short time—perhaps a few hours, perhaps a few days. She was probably baptized at home by her parents, which the Church allows when the newborn's life is in danger. It is not known where she is buried because she is not listed in any cemetery or parish records.

Emilia named her baby after her older sister, whom she had loved so much. That sister's death at the age of twenty-two was one of the sorrows that marked Emilia's childhood, followed shortly by the intense grief of her mother's death at the age of thirty-nine.

The loss of little Olga left a profound mark on Emilia. The pain was so great that she hardly ever spoke about the baby girl—only on rare occasions with people she knew well. Her neighbor Maria Janina said that any time Emilia remembered her baby's death, she seemed to experience tremendous pain all over again.

In fact, Emilia never shared the details about Olga's death nor even the date she died. The tiny body was not included when a family vault was erected in Kraków. When the Wojtyla home in Wadowice was transformed into a museum, little Olga's name was not inscribed on the family plaque at the entrance.

Following this difficult pregnancy, Emilia was prone to severe back pain, which eventually prevented her standing. In addition, she began to experience sudden dizziness that would make her lose consciousness. Whenever one of these spells occurred, she had to stay in bed for four or five days in a row. At times she would need to be transported to Kraków to be treated by specialists. Her times away could last for a week. Her husband would do the household errands, feed Edmund, wash the dishes and clean the house. The doctors said Emilia had damaged kidneys and a weak heart. They advised her to live a quiet and tranquil life. She should avoid tiring herself out. And of course, she could not ever contemplate another pregnancy.

MAY 18, 1920

In 1919 the family rented a small second-story apartment with a garden on 2 Rynek Street, which has become 7 Kościelna Street and is now a John Paul II museum. The windows looked out on the gray wall of the parish church across the street, St. Mary's. On that wall, next to the sundial, were the words "Time flies; eternity remains." The church was so close to the Wojtyla apartment that when the windows were open, the family could hear the prayers and the singing during services.

At the end of 1919 Emilia discovered she was expecting another baby. She was already thirty-five and a half years old, and this new pregnancy was immediately difficult. The doctors told her that both she and the baby would die and that she should end the pregnancy.

The problem was certainly serious. Emilia understood the status of her health and certainly would have thought about the doctors' advice. She knew the risks and thought about Edmund, who was fourteen at that time, about her husband and about herself. It is not easy to accept death at age thirty-five.

If Emilia had listened to the doctors, we would never have had a pope called Karol Wojtyla. But Emilia was a woman of faith. With great simplicity she entrusted herself to God's goodness. She would not prevent this baby's birth for any reason in the world; as for herself, she was prepared to die.

The baby's birth on May 18, 1920, was difficult, but he was healthy and sound. It was a Wednesday, and he was born around sunset. Karol himself has told friends that when the delivery was over, his mother asked the midwife to open the bedroom windows. The sounds of church bells and Marian choruses, being sung in the church in honor of Our Lady during the evening May services, were the first sounds the future pope heard on entering this world.

But that same day he also was exposed to the patriotic enthusiasm of his father. Together with the whole country, Lieutenant Wojtyla was celebrating the victory of Marshal Józef Pilsudski, who was returning with his troops to Warsaw after soundly defeating Lenin's Red Army in Kiev, Ukraine, during the war for Polish independence. According to some people, the father gave baby Karol the middle name of Józef in order to honor Marshal Pilsudski. Others say the name Józef was in honor of the Emperor, Franz Joseph. Emilia liked to call her sons diminutive and endearing names, so she called the child Lolek or Lolus.

THE FIRST SACRAMENT

The baby was baptized a month later, on June 20, 1920. The parish church record in Wadowice reads:

> Birth certificate and baptismal certificate. In the year of Our Lord one thousand, nine hundred and twenty (1920) on the eighteenth day (18) of the month of May, Carolus Josephus, a member of the Catholic faith, of the male sex and from a legitimate marriage, was born at residence #2 and baptized on the 20th day of June of this same year according to the Roman Catholic rite by Most Reverend Franciszek Zak. Father: Carolus Wojtyla, an army officer, son of Matthew and Anna Przeczka. Mother: Emilia Kaczorowska, daughter of Felice and Maria Scholz. Godparents: Józef Kuczmierczyk, Maria Wiadrwoska, wife of Leon.

Maria was Emilia's sister. The two sisters knew Józef Kuczmierczyk for two reasons: He had married their older sister, Olga, and after being widowed, he married their other sister, Melena-Augusta. Józef Kuczmierczyk was well off. He owned a famous restaurant in Kraków that was frequented by devoted and important clientele. His most famous clients were the author Ludwik Solski and the playwright Stanislaw Wyspiański, a greatly esteemed artist.

John Paul II has often recalled the date and place of his baptism and said that he thought of the parish as his native environment. On June 20, 1920, his family took him to the baptismal font of the church in Wadowice for his baptism. When he was archbishop of Kraków, he returned and solemnly kissed that font during the millennium of Poland's christening. On the fiftieth anniversary of his baptism, when he was a cardinal, he visited Wadowice and again kissed the baptismal font. As pope, he returned one more time to the church in Wadowice and kissed the font where he received, as he said, the grace to become a son of God and to have faith in the Redeemer.

A Loving Family

Lolek grew up healthy and robust. As a young boy he had a joyful, lively and extroverted personality.

Emilia's life, in contrast, seemed seriously in danger. This third pregnancy had been very damaging. Her heart and kidney conditions grew worse. Her legs swelled and prevented her from being able to stand for any length of time.

She nevertheless still had to take care of the house and her sons. Now that the family had grown, the work at home increased, and her husband's salary was no longer sufficient. Even as her energy was decreasing, Emilia felt it her duty to contribute to the family income. She dusted off her sewing machine and took in work from neighbors.

Edmund, who was fourteen years older than Karol, attended high school in Wadowice, but in the afternoon he would help his mother at home. Every day Emilia would take a short walk, pushing Lolek's carriage. Edmund would help her take the carriage down the stairs from their apartment and clear the path if it was blocked; he would push the carriage himself whenever he saw that his mother was tired. Every so often Emilia had to stay in the hospital, and then it was up to Edmund to look after his brother.

In 1924 Edmund graduated at the head of his high school class and enrolled in the university at Kraków. Despite the economic difficulties at home, his parents were proud of him and wanted their son to continue his studies. He dreamed of becoming a doctor because medicine was a profession that helped people who were suffering.

With Edmund's departure all of the tasks in the house fell to Emilia. It was a heavy burden that she carried quietly.

Karol Sr. asked for early retirement in 1927 because his presence was necessary at home. The army sent him into retirement with a promotion to captain because of meritorious conduct. From that time on people in Wadowice referred to him with great respect as "the captain." However, despite the prestigious title, the captain's pension was lower than his working salary had been, and so the family had to make other sacrifices. Karol did not complain because he needed to be near his wife.

SCHOOL DAYS

Meanwhile, little Lolek started attending the local elementary school. This was located on the second floor of the city's administration building in the market square, about a minute's walk from his house. From the beginning he was clearly a very gifted student. He had some trouble with math, but he eventually overcame that. His report card after the first semester of first grade has been preserved:

> Behavior: Very good
>
> Motivation: Good
>
> Religion: Very good

Polish language: Good

Mathematics: Good

Drawing: Good

Singing: Very Good

Gym: Very good

Absences: 20, all excused

The absences were because of his mother's health. Whenever Emilia was bedridden and her husband could not be home because of his work, little Lolek had to stay home and help his mother in whatever way he could. This was another reason the senior Karol Wojtyla asked for retirement in 1927: He did not want his young son to miss so much school.

Lolek made friends at school with Jerzy Kluger, the son of the president of the Hebrew community in Wadowice, a well-known lawyer. The two boys became inseparable, and their friendship has lasted to this day.

Jerzy Kluger recounts that they always played near the town square, about a block from the Wojtylas' apartment. There they often saw Cwick, the policeman in their area. One day, when they were six or seven years old, they were discussing the policeman's sword. Lolek insisted that it was made of wood, while Jerzy said it was steel. The policeman was dozing on a bench near them, so they decided to investigate. They approached him, trying to take the long sword out of its sheath, but they lost their balance and fell on top of Cwick. He woke up with a jolt and sent the two boys running.

Lolek's times with Jerzy were usually more peaceful. Now and then he would go to Jerzy's house, where Jerzy's grandmother, who had taken a liking to Lolek, would serve tea and cake. But these visits were rare because he didn't want to be away from his mother, who needed him more and more.

EMILIA'S LAST DAYS

Anyone could see that Emilia's health was getting worse. She tried to hide her illnesses so as not to be a burden, but she was suffering a great deal. Her neighbor Maria Janina Kaczorowa remembers Emilia's last years. In 1985, when she was eighty-four, Maria Janina spoke at length about Emilia to Roman Antonj Gajczak. She allowed her comments to be recorded, and the significant details she furnished were given to the Italian Catholic writer Luciano Bergonzoni for his book on the pope's mother:

> We lived on the same street.
>
> Emilia was a very peaceful, well-educated person.... She was very joyful and lived according to God's will even when she was sick. I don't know what her illnesses were; I never knew because I never allowed myself to ask her. I guessed heart problems and rheumatism. There were times when she couldn't stand, but I didn't dare ask her about it because she was older than I was.
>
> She bore her suffering through faith. She never spoke about her problems, and she always had a sweet and peaceful smile, even at her times of greatest suffering. We would talk about everything, the way neighbors do, but especially about Karol, whom she loved so much. She was disappointed that she was so ill.
>
> She dressed very modestly, mostly in pastel colors. She had long, slightly graying hair, which she wore piled on top of her head, since that was the fashion then. Her voice was pleasant and calm. Sometimes I would say to Mrs. Emilia, "Please stop me if I talk too much or too fast." She would answer, "You're fine; don't worry." She was a very quiet person, but a very feminine one.
>
> I can't say that she was a woman of few words. She was a very educated, typical woman of her time. She was very well liked: Even people who didn't know her would recognize her inner peace and her religious nature.
>
> She would say to me, "Mrs. Janina, you are very young, but there is a moment that comes when people must resign themselves to their misfortunes." Emilia was sorrowful because she had lost her little girl, Olga. No one knows very much about that

incident…. I don't know if the baby died after birth or was still-born. I never dared to ask about it.

I have a daughter, and Mrs. Wojtyla knew how much I loved my little girl—and I thank God that she is still alive today. I told her once that my firstborn, a son, had died. She asked me how it happened, so I told her everything about his illness and death. She was very moved and tried to console me, saying, "You'll see, you'll have another son…," and that's exactly what ended up happening.

Someone saw Emilia when they took her away to the hospital for the last time. She couldn't stand up anymore, and she had terrible back pain. In Wadowice people said she had either spinal or heart problems. Then she died.[2]

"OH, MOTHER, MY DEPARTED LOVE"

The terrible tragedy occurred on April 13, 1929. That morning Lolek, who was not quite nine, got up early as usual to go to school. His mother, despite her pain, prepared his breakfast, then kissed and hugged him before he went out the door. Perhaps she sensed that she might never see him again.

At midday someone went to school to speak to the principal. When the principal went to the third-grade room, all the boys stood up. He spoke to the teacher, who turned to Karol Wojtyla and motioned to him that he should go with the principal. The boy turned pale and said nothing.

Outside the school a neighbor lady was waiting for him. "Your mother was taken to the hospital, but unfortunately she died," said the woman. The boy returned with her in silence to his home.

Emilia was forty-five years old. Her death certificate listed the cause of death as myocarditis (inflammation of the heart) and nephritis (inflammation of the kidneys). The funeral took place on April 16.

No one knows the pain little Lolek experienced. His mother's death caused such trauma for him that he lost many memories of her. In his book *Gift and Mystery* he wrote:

I had not yet made my First Holy Communion when I lost my mother: I was barely nine years old. So I do not have a clear awareness of her contribution, which must have been great, to my religious training.[3]

All of Karol Wojtyla's friends agree that he almost could not bring himself to speak of his mother. Only once did he confide to his friend, the French journalist André Frossard, "My mother's death made a deep impression on my memory." [4]

His tender and continuing love for his mother is demonstrated by the fact that he still has several items that belonged to her, including a small table and a wicker basket that she used for laundry. On a table in his bedroom—whether at the Vatican or at Castel Gandolfo—he keeps a small photograph of his mother standing next to his father, taken shortly after their wedding.

In 1939, ten years after his mother's death, he had become a confirmed poet. He wrote in remembrance of his mother a gentle prayer full of deep sorrow:

> Over this your white grave
> the flowers of life in white—
> so many years without you—
> how many have passed out of sight?
> Over this your white grave
> covered for years, there is a stir
> in the air, something uplifting
> and, like death, beyond comprehension.
> Over this your white grave
> Oh, mother, can such loving cease?
> For all his filial adoration
> a prayer:
> Give her eternal peace—[5]

CHAPTER THREE

The Captain's School

THE LOSS OF KAROL'S mother presented a situation that can be somewhat dangerous for a youngster. Psychologists and educators agree that in order for to grow up healthy, children need a maternal presence. Lolek's teachers, neighbors and relatives noticed that he changed. He rarely spoke, he did not go to school, and he did not like to play anymore.

We can assume that the enemy sought to take advantage of this situation to damage the child's emotional equilibrium. Satan would have liked this young boy to lose faith in himself, in others and in God and to become withdrawn, lonely, sad and pessimistic. This would have profoundly affected his character as an adult.

But our heavenly mother was watching over Lolek. Emilia was also watching over him with even greater power than before. One can imagine that the two mothers worked together, inspiring Captain Wojtyla to make the right decisions about the boy.

The captain was a reserved man. Because of the discipline of military training, he did not show his emotions easily. The sorrow over the loss of his wife was so intense that his hair turned white in a matter of weeks. Nevertheless, he could not think about himself; he needed to focus on his sons, especially the younger one.

PILGRIMAGE

First he sought help through prayer. He decided to make a pilgrimage with his sons to the Marian shrine at Kalwaria Zebrzydowska, where Our Lady is venerated as the patron of Poland. This is the Polish shrine *par excellence*, the holiest place in Poland, a kind of Polish "Jerusalem." It is located in the foothills of the Bieszczady Mountains, about six miles from Wadowice on the way to Kraków, and it holds powerful symbolism.

The outdoor shrine consists of a basilica, dedicated to the Holy Cross, which was built in 1658 at the top of Kalwaria by Cistercian monks, and forty-six chapels in the fields and woods, all connected by footpaths. Twenty-four of these chapels are dedicated to different events in Jesus' earthly life, while twenty-one are dedicated to events in Our Lady's life. The two paths, the "Way of Our Lord" and the "Way of Our Lady," wind through the vast area, each following its own direction, but they intersect at the largest chapel, dedicated to Mary's assumption. This signifies the fact that through Mary a person can reach the kingdom promised by Jesus. Every spring a passion play is performed, and in August a mystery play commemorates the death and assumption of the Blessed Virgin into heaven. On the eve of the Assumption, August 14, tens of thousands of pilgrims accompany a wooden statue of the Blessed Virgin in procession to the tomb. They keep watch through the night, singing and praying, and the next day they celebrate her triumph over death. Every Polish family makes the pilgrimage to the shrine of Kalwaria at least once a year. Little Lolek would naturally have visited this place earlier with his parents. John Paul II specifically referred to it during his first trip to Poland after being elected pope:

> I really do not know how to thank Divine Providence for granting me [the opportunity] to revisit this place: Kalwaria Zebrzydowska, the shrine of the Mother of God.... I visited [this shrine] often as a boy and as a young man...as a priest. Especially, I often visited the Shrine of Kalwaria as Archbishop of Kraków and Cardinal. Many times we came here, the priests and I, to concelebrate before the Mother of God.[1]

The captain wanted to bring his sons to this holy place so that they could meditate and reflect and find strength to deal with their very great sorrow. He felt that he did not have the right words to explain the meaning of the tragedy that had befallen their family. His sons needed to do more than weep for what had happened; they also needed to hope and to understand the invisible spiritual reality. The captain thought that with prayer in this holy place, perhaps his words would have a force and a clarity that could transmit to his sons the truth he believed but whose fullness he had difficulty communicating.

A DOMESTIC SEMINARY

Edmund returned to Kraków for his medical studies. Lolek returned to his third-grade class in Wadowice. The captain stayed home to carry out the duties that his wife had formerly fulfilled.

It was customary at that time for widowers to remarry. Emilia's father had remarried, and so had Karol's brother-in-law Józef Kuczmierczyk. The captain probably thought about that possibility but decided against it. No one would take Emilia's place in his home.

He suspected that Lolek would be a special child. Parents often have these kinds of intuitions. The captain decided to dedicate himself to his son. No one could have helped, understood or guided the child the way he could. He rolled up his sleeves, pushed aside his own great sorrow and, in his usual style, made a plan. For twelve years, from 1929 to 1941, Karol Wojtyla Sr. was father, mother, friend, teacher, role model and playmate for Lolek. The two became inseparable.

For people who did not know him, this retired officer could seem a bit strange. His life was very private. He hardly spoke to anyone and hardly ever left the house. But those who knew him well understood that he was sacrificing every moment of his life so that little Lolek would grow up well.

He set up a kind of religious community life with his son, following a strict schedule. They would get up at 7:00 A.M., attend Mass at the parish church and eat breakfast. Lolek would go to school, and Karol would clean the house, do the laundry, mend the clothes and cook. In the afternoon Lolek would play with his friends for two hours and then return to study with his father. In the early evening they would go to church together again, have dinner, take a short walk and then go to bed.

Every so often, especially during winter evenings when they could not walk outdoors, they stayed home and had long discussions. The captain would talk about Polish history and literature and would read his son poetry, which they would then comment on together. He taught little Lolek German and tailor-made a Polish-German dictionary for him. He taught him German so well that when he was in high school, Karol Jr. was able to read Kant's *Critique of Pure Reason* in the original, much to the astonishment of both his friends and professors.

They lived in a wonderful atmosphere of mutual understanding and affection. Their days together were never boring, sad or melancholic. The captain was a very attentive, generous and selfless man, and he knew how to adapt to the needs of his son. Although he talked about history and literature, he also talked about sports, music and entertainment. Often the father and son would go to the movies together, which Lolek particularly enjoyed. On Sundays they would eat lunch together in a restaurant and take a long walk along the Skawa River.

They also played together. Zbigniew Silkowski, one of Lolek's peers, recalled that sometimes when he would go visit his friend, he could hear a lot of commotion in the house with shouts and running footsteps. On entering the apartment, he would find both father and son all sweaty, playing soccer with a ball made of rags.

SPIRITUAL MENTORS

Karol was an incomparable mentor of spiritual life for his son. Lolek's schoolmates state that they would often see the two Wojtylas kneeling next to one another in church, engrossed in prayer. It was a moving sight.

The Holy Father, in his writings, preserves the extreme reserve that characterized his family matters, but he has given us a description of his father that is a genuine memorial. He confided to his friend, André Frossard:

> My father was admirable, and almost all the memories of my childhood and adolescence are connected with him. The violence of the blows which had struck him had opened up immense spiritual depths in him; his grief found its outlet in prayer. The mere fact of seeing him on his knees had a decisive influence on my early years. He was so hard on himself that he had no need to be hard on his son; his example alone was sufficient to inculcate discipline and a sense of duty. He was an exceptional person.[2]

In his book *Gift and Mystery* he writes that his childhood memories are mostly of his father:

> [He was] a deeply religious man.
>
> Day after day I was able to observe the austere way in which he lived. By profession he was a soldier and, after my mother's death, his life became one of constant prayer. Sometimes I would wake up during the night and find my father on his knees, just as I would see him kneeling in the parish church. We never spoke about a vocation to the priesthood, but *his example was in a way my first seminary*, a kind of domestic seminary.[3]

Lolek had another solid example, support and teacher: his older brother. Edmund had been on hand to help little Lolek when his mother was alive. After Emilia's death Edmund understood the psychological stress that his little brother was experiencing, so he took Lolek under his wing. He became an ideal companion. Just as the father was also a mother to Lolek, Edmund became Lolek's friend, example and guide. When he would come home from school, instead of thinking about himself, his friends, girlfriends and entertainment, he would commit his time to Lolek.

Edmund was a twenty-three-year-old medical student when his mother died. All the people who knew him well agree that he was a very intelligent, healthy, strong, stable, obedient and religious young man. One person described him as a young man full of energy, with blond hair and blue eyes, who looked like an athlete. He was a reliable, well-educated, charming and good-humored young man who loved to play tennis, soccer, bridge and chess.

"Edmund looked like his father," said Maria Janina, their neighbor. "He was robust and masculine. He had pensive eyes and was very calm and even-tempered. He was irreproachable in everything he did."[4]

Lolek adored his older brother and wanted to be just like him when he grew up. Neighbors say that whenever Edmund

came home from Kraków for vacations, the two were inseparable. Edmund would play soccer with his little brother and
would carry him on his shoulders through the countryside.
Edmund passed on to Lolek his enthusiasm for outdoor life,
his love of nature and his passion for hiking and skiing.
With the help of his brother and father, Lolek regained confidence in himself and in life. He did not forget his mother, but
he succeeded in overcoming the depression he had fallen into
immediately after losing her. Indeed, the sorrow always per-
sisted and was very great. One day when he was a cardinal, he
told his friend Frossard, "[B]oys brought up by their
father...make the painful discovery that they have been
deprived of a mother."[5] He recognized that deprivation but
without being traumatized, thanks to the extraordinary love
of the captain and Edmund.

HOLY MOTHERS
The absence of a mother helped him, little by little, become
aware of Our Lady's presence in people's lives. He was still very
young, but there are no age constraints for communication
between mother and son and between the "heavenly Mother"
and her sons in this world. Thus he developed a devotion to
Our Lady.

In addition, his long deliberations on his mother's situation
helped him to develop a special sensitivity to problems that
women and mothers have concerning motherhood and life in
general. The role of women, and in particular their dedication
to motherhood, has been one of his major pastoral themes.
His opposition to abortion and his determination to protect
the unborn are obviously tied to his own experience. Every
time he praises mothers who die so that their babies can live,
one can hear an echo of the tragedy that marked his
own life.

On April 14, 1995, the pope beatified an Italian woman, Giovanna Beretta Molla, a pediatrician who faced something similar to what his mother faced. While she was pregnant with her fourth child, she developed a tumor, but she chose to carry her child to term rather than have an abortion, which would probably have saved her life. When he spoke of Dr. Beretta Molla, John Paul II's eyes filled and his voice trembled.

The magnificent upbringing under the captain and Edmund brought great strength and understanding to little Lolek. All of this, however, was not pleasing to the "enemy," who would have used the mother's death to damage the young boy. Seeing himself defeated, Satan tried to deliver a different blow.

ANOTHER DANGER

Often, especially on holidays, the captain would have lunch with his son at a nearby restaurant. He was a friend of the owner, Alojzy Banaś, and his wife, Maria. Lolek liked to play with their son Boguslaw, who was only a few years older. After lunch the captain would stay to chat with the restaurant owners while the two boys played.

The policeman in that district was a regular patron at the restaurant, where he would go drink a few beers when his shift was over. Sometimes he would linger for a long time, and if he realized he had had too much to drink, he would ask the restaurant owner to keep his gun for him. He would usually remove the bullets before handing it over. Mr. Banaś would smile and put the gun in the drawer where he kept his money. The next day the policeman would come back to get his gun.

Boguslaw Banaś was fascinated by the weapon. He liked to look at it, touch it and hold it in his hand. He had to be secretive about this because his parents had told him several times that he absolutely should not go anywhere near the gun.

One Sunday afternoon Boguslaw, taking advantage of the fact that no one was in the restaurant, decided to show the weapon to his friend Karol Wojtyla. The two of them sneaked into the restaurant. Boguslaw headed for the drawer and, beaming with pride, took the gun out to show his friend.

Boguslaw wanted to show that he knew how to use the gun. Expecting it to be unloaded, he aimed the weapon at Karol: "Stick up your hands or I'll shoot," he said, smiling, and pulled the trigger. A loud explosion ripped through the air.

Boguslaw's parents, Karol's father and the other people who were talking outside the restaurant all came running. The two boys were white as ghosts. The bullet had grazed Lolck's head and had lodged in the wall. The shot had been fired from a little over three feet away, and everyone was convinced that only a miracle prevented the bullet from hitting its target.

CHAPTER FOUR

Edmund's Sacrifice ✝

THE YEAR 1930 WAS a very important one for Lolek. He turned ten at the end of May. In June he finished elementary school with the highest grades and was admitted into middle school. In July he made his first trip to Kraków with his father, to attend his brother Edmund's graduation from medical school.

The trip inspired Lolek with new ideas. He was awed by the stately old Collegium Majus, where the medical school was housed. He attended the solemn services with pride, eyes fixed on his brother and the professors in their academic garb. He applauded enthusiastically with the professors, the students and his relatives when Edmund's degree was conferred magna cum laude.

Even the captain had tears in his eyes. He was perhaps thinking how happy his wife Emilia would have been, because she had been the one to insist that her son graduate from college. Edmund's reaching that goal with academic honors brought great satisfaction to the family.

Edmund's education was also an excellent investment for the future. With his son a doctor, the captain, who had retired on a meager stipend, could face the future with some tranquility. His son could help provide for him in his old age and help secure little Lolek's future.

Also in 1930 Lolek became an altar boy. That same year a young priest, Father Kazimierz Figlewicz, arrived in Wadowice. He was responsible for the altar boys and taught catechism at the middle school. He came to know Lolek well, both as the overseer of the altar boys and as his religion teacher. He also became Lolek's confessor and spiritual director, continuing in that role until Karol became a priest.

Recalling those years in Wadowice, Kazimierz Figlewicz said:

> As a young priest, I was the vicar in the parish at Wadowice. In 1930 I taught religion in the middle school. It was there that I began my long acquaintance with the student Karol Wojtyla. At age ten, Karol was fairly tall but a bit plump. He was a lively, quick-witted, intelligent, good boy. He was optimistic by nature because, as I observed him closely, the cloud of sadness due to his mother's premature death lifted in less than a year. I also observed that he was loyal in his relationships with classmates; he was never involved in conflicts with any teachers and he was very good at his studies.[1]

Dr. Edmund Wojtyla had a lofty ideal: He wanted to dedicate himself to people who were suffering, not only because it was his professional duty now but also because it was a Christian vocation, an idea his mother had taught him. His graduation thesis was called *Repercussions of Illness on Coronary Arteries*. He chose to continue studying this topic and to specialize in cardiology. This would have required more years of sacrifice, but he would have become a very famous doctor.

Edmund attended classes at the Pediatric Clinic of Kraków and began his internship at the hospital in Bielsko, Silesia, as an assistant in cardiology. He did not have much free time, especially since he was passionate about his work and dedicated to his patients. Yet, times with his family became more frequent. When he could, Edmund would go back to Wadowice to be with his father and his brother, and Lolek and the captain would frequently visit Edmund at his hospital.

Everything was going well. The Wojtyla family was getting over their sorrow at the loss of Emilia. Edmund was the pride of the hospital in Bielsko where he worked. Lolek was the best student in the high school for boys in Wadowice, Marcin Wadowita.

The captain, reserved and silent, marveled at these two wonderful boys who gave him so much satisfaction. He was ready to help them by carrying out all the humble but necessary household tasks that are generally the mother's work. Most of all, he prayed and thanked the Lord for the gift of his sons and for such a peaceful life.

A NEW SORROW

At the end of November in 1932, a young girl named Anna was admitted to the hospital at Bielsko. She was twenty-one years old and had scarlet fever. This is an infectious disease that can be transmitted by a sick person as well as a healthy one. At that time it was fatal because antibiotics did not exist. Every hospital had an isolated section for people with the disease; medical assistance was almost nonexistent, left to charitable volunteers.

When Anna was hospitalized in Bielsko, she was put in isolation and practically abandoned. No doctor wanted to care for her since the danger of contamination was so high. Nurses were in charge of her minimal care.

Dr. Edmund Wojtyla thought this treatment was unjust. He thought it was absurd to leave sick people to themselves, at the mercy of atrocious pain, only because of fear of contagion. He freely offered to help the young girl.

He understood clearly the serious risk that he faced. He also knew that he had no professional obligation toward this girl because she was not his patient and she was not part of the cardiology unit where he was working. But he upheld his duty as a doctor—a duty founded in altruism and Christian conscience—not to abandon someone who was seriously ill.

According to stories published in the newspapers, Dr. Edmund Wojtyla did his utmost to help this young girl. He remained at her side day and night, even when it was clear that nothing more could be done. He stayed with her to comfort her and to allay her fears as she faced death.

When Edmund realized he was infected with the disease, it was already too late.

Lolek came home from school to be greeted one more time by a sober-faced person, who told him point-blank that his brother was about to die. Once again he saw his father's pained expression and his eyes swollen from weeping.

They left together for the hospital in Bielsko. It was a silent and very painful journey, and at the hospital they faced the most unexpected tragedy that could be imagined. Edmund, the robust and healthy young man, always smiling and selfless, was dying. His medical colleagues tried to help, but the disease could not be treated.

The captain and Lolek could not go near their beloved Edmund because of the danger of infection. For three days Edmund was in horrible agony. For three days the captain and Lolek stayed outside the quarantined room, weeping, unable to give any comfort to their loved one. Edmund died on the evening of December 4, 1932.

Newspaper columns noted the death of the young doctor. One headline read, "Death of a Doctor in the Line of Duty." A

long article in the popular newspaper *Itaco* told of Dr.
Wojtyla's passion for medicine and his wonderful bedside
manner.

The managing directors of the hospital in Bielsko posted
the following announcement inside the hospital and around
the city:

> Dr. Edmund Wojtyla, age twenty-six, assistant at the Community
> Hospital in Bielsko, came to rest in the arms of Our Lord at 7:00
> P.M. on December 4, 1932, after receiving Extreme Unction and
> offering his young life for suffering humanity. Greatly saddened
> by the loss of our dear colleague and beloved coworker, let us pray
> to the Almighty that his soul may rest in peace.

LAID TO REST

The newspaper reports deeply moved the population of
Bielsko. A large crowd attended the funeral on December 6.

Before the casket was lowered into the ground, some people offered a few words. Among them was Dr. Bruckner, one of
the doctors who had tried to treat their colleague. His speech,
possibly considered old-fashioned rhetoric today, made clear
how extraordinary this young man was:

> Although you were not a soldier bearing weapons, you are a hero.
> You are a martyr in your youth because you were struck down
> waging a battle against death. It has conquered you, it has you in
> its ice-cold grip because, dear colleague, you dared to attempt to
> rescue a young girl from its jaws. You have left us forever.... From
> your early days you went through the hard school of life and now
> have begun to work and to understand the saying by the poet
> Mickiewicz, "Let my poems die, and let the readers then gather
> the fruit of understanding from them." A mysterious event has
> happened for which the Omnipotent, and not the people, will
> judge you. In the battle against death, against serious disease, in
> that hellish dance with death, your dying glance looked to us for
> help. I still see your suffering face, I still hear your feverish lips
> whispering right up to the last moment, "Why me?"[2]

Edmund's last words reveal how great his pain and dismay must have been. He had already suffered much during his life. He had sacrificed himself selflessly because of his lofty, altruistic goals. But the Lord came to take him, even though he was only twenty-six, and Edmund was not able to understand.

When he was in perfect health, he often said, "True prayer is waiting for God to come when and how He wants to." That is a profound statement full of evangelical wisdom, but in reality, when God does come and death shows itself, the dismay can be immense. Even Jesus cried out on the cross, "My God, why have you forsaken me?"

On December 22 the city council of Bielsko officially commemorated Edmund Wojtyla in a public meeting through a speech by the mayor, Dr. Kobiela. After recounting the young doctor's tragic end and the story of his life and professional achievements, the mayor said:

> Dr. Wojtyla was always happy to help his patients not only through his medical knowledge, which he sought to deepen through more study, but by standing by them as a friend because he was very much loved and respected. The city of Bielsko has lost an excellent doctor because of the premature death of Dr. Wojtyla—someone whom they could have expected a lot from. We will never forget him, his sacrificial work, his gifts and his wonderful character. We salute his memory![3]

Captain Wojtyla and Lolek appreciated all the expressions of condolences they received. Even if people's sympathy did not relieve their pain, it was nonetheless a sign of great esteem and affection. After the services they in turn expressed public thanks through a statement in the newspapers:

> We, father and son, express heartfelt thanks to all the people who extended assistance and consideration, despite the danger to their own lives and health, during the illness of our late family member, Dr. Edmund, a doctor at the city hospital in Bielsko, Silesia. We wish to express thanks from the bottom of our hearts to the

doctors of that hospital… [and] to the kind nurses…. We want to thank those who took part in the funeral services for Edmund: the pastor, Father Kaperlik; the prefect, Dr. Bochenski; the mayor, Dr. Kobiela; the representatives of the City Council of Bielsko; the hospital director, Dr. Reinprecht; Dr. Walach, the president of the Polish Circle and Dr. Popiolek, the president of the Polish Choir; the nursing staff, the employees and personnel at the hospital; and all those who attended the funeral. We express thanks for the funeral eulogies spoken over Edmund's grave by Father Kasperlik, Dr. Bruckner and Dr. Walach.

When they returned to their apartment in Wadowice, Lolek and the captain were heartbroken. In the comfort of their home, they held each other tightly and abandoned themselves to a flood of tears. Only three years had elapsed since the mother's death, and now Edmund was gone. The family had been cut in half. Only their deep faith and prayer prevented their sorrow from turning into despair.

This bereavement also left an indelible mark on little Lolek's heart. At school the young boy went back to being sad. Father Edward Zacher went to Wadowice in December, 1932, to teach religion in the middle school. He asked about the boy with the sad but intelligent face and others told him that he was Lolek Wojtyla and that he was sad because his only brother had just died.

After he became pope, Karol Wojtyla, comparing the deaths of his mother and his brother, said to his friend André Frossard, "My brother's [death]…perhaps [made] a still deeper [impression] because of the dramatic circumstances in which it occurred and because I was more mature."[4]

LESSONS FROM EDMUND

Edmund Wojtyla was a selfless doctor and a believer ready to help his neighbor in God's name, but he was also a doctor who was socially committed and concerned with the problems of the poor. He sought solutions that were fair and practical. He was, in fact, a forerunner in the field of social medicine. Edmund Wojtyla was part of an avant-garde movement in his time. Inspired by the gospel, he was committed to providing for the less privileged. In fact, with several friends he was doing his best in the hospital at Bielsko to set up a special unit for the working class, the poor and the disenfranchised. He was also committed to sharing the ideas he believed in. He had summarized these in an article for a publication that was interested in social issues:

Social medicine is a discipline that arises from the necessity, for the sake of public health, to integrate hygiene and health care. It requires an understanding of the interaction of human beings and their social environment.

Every individual, in fact, cannot be considered in a vacuum— as a mere abstraction—divorced from the social sphere in which that person lives. Each person needs to be seen as someone who receives continuous physical and psychic stimuli from a variety of social factors (economic, professional, familial, hereditary, etc.). These factors can have a distinct influence on a person's health, and each person has to somehow adapt to them.

Therefore, social medicine studies the links between health and a person's social environment and focuses on the individual as well as the group. It seeks to prevent the harmful effects of a social environment on health and to develop healthy practices for the social class to which an individual belongs. In the last analysis, social medicine includes the preventative, educational, and therapeutic aspects of medicine as well as the expertise of the doctors and the political, economic, and legal resources that can serve public health.[5]

Karol Wojtyla never forgot Edmund's herosim. In 1992, when he was presented a booklet that outlined Edmund Wojtyla's life, John Paul II immediately kissed the cover photograph. He has always kept his brother's stethoscope in a drawer of his desk as a precious treasure. These are indications

of how attached John Paul II still is to the memory
of Edmund.

CHAPTER FIVE

"The Ballad of Spring" ✝

IN 1934 FOURTEEN-YEAR-OLD Karol Wojtyla suddenly discovered theater.

For some time he had been aware of the Romantic literature of Poland. During the long winter nights his father would read him entire works of poetry and fiction, and the two would often engage in lively dialogue, commenting on and digging deeply into the texts.

Lolek's favorite author at that time was Henryk Sienkiewicz, the Nobel Prize winner for literature in 1906. He was the author of, among other things, the famous story *Quo Vadis?*, a moving evocation of early Christianity in Nero's Rome during the time of persecution. The captain had read the whole novel to his son, as well as other important works by Sienkiewicz, in particular the famous trilogy *With Fire and Sword, The Deluge* and *Mr. Wolodyjowski.* This comprised a lengthy narrative about the period of turmoil in Polish history between 1648 and 1673, during the time of the Cossack wars, the Swedish invasion and the wars with Turkey. Lolek was moved by the glorious exploits in defense of the faith and the fatherland.

Along with the works by Sienkiewicz, the captain introduced his son to the works of such poet-playwrights of the Polish Romantic movement as Adam Mickiewicz, a patriot who was a friend of Alexander Pushkin; Juliusz Slowacki; and Cyprian Kamil Norwid, a friend of Frederick Chopin. Still an adolescent, Lolek knew some of these authors' works by heart: Mickiewicz' *Pan Tadeusz*, Slowacki's *Kordian* and Norwid's *Promethidion*. He liked to recite these works at home or with friends who also loved Romantic literature.

In 1934 his fertile imagination was drawn to the performing arts, especially the dramas that were being staged. That attention transformed into a total and absolute passion.

At that time Wadowice enjoyed the reputation of being one of the most active cultural centers in Poland. It had professional and amateur theater companies that were producing quality works in public locales, in theaters, in schools, in parish recreation centers and even in private homes.

Lolek became an avid theatergoer. He would see plays with his father after having read and studied their texts at home. Before long he became personally involved in the staging of these works.

ON STAGE

It was customary in Wadowice for schools to have their own acting groups, which periodically would put on plays. In 1935 the Marcin Wadowita School, which Lolek was attending, collaborated with the Moscicka School for Girls to stage *Antigone*, the ancient Greek tragedy by Sophocles. Lolek played the protagonist, showing great promise as an actor, and from that time on his stage commitments followed in a steady stream and became increasingly significant. These roles were not only with his school's acting group but also with professional theater companies like those at his church.

Lolek's acting improved with practice. He had a deep voice, an elegant and refined stance and an innate capacity to give depth and meaning to the texts. His reputation spread beyond his city, as the acting troupe he was part of was invited to other cities. Important people connected to the national theater came to Wadowice to observe Karol Wojtyla.

His passion for the theater grew beyond acting. He began to do stage direction, to plan stage sets and to choose the texts that would be presented. He became the director of his school theater group.

He had a prodigious memory. In the spring of 1937 Wojtyla's group was performing Slowacki's *Balladyna* (*Ballad of Spring*), a play in which the author mixes characters and scenes from old Polish ballads and from famous dramas like *Macbeth*, *King Lear* and *Midsummer Night's Dream*. Wojtyla was playing the part of Kirbor, the protagonist.

Two days before the play was to open, the actor playing the part of Kostryn, a role almost as important as that of the protagonist, had to drop out. It was impossible to find a substitute in twenty-four hours. After so much work and effort, the play would need to be cancelled. All the people involved were very disappointed and disheartened, but Karol saved the day.

"In the play," he said to his group, "Kostryn enters on stage after Kirbor, my character, has died, so I can play the part of Kostryn too."

"But how arc you going to learn it in twenty-four hours?" asked his puzzled companions.

"I already know it," he answered. "I learned it during rehearsals."

The play went ahead as planned. Karol played the two roles very successfully, and his reputation as an actor saw a meteoric rise.

MANY TALENTS

It was not only theater that Karol was passionate about during this time. He was attracted to anything that qualified as art, poetry or music. He wrote poetry and songs. He had a passionate, romantic soul.

Karol was not a child anymore; he had become a tall, healthy young man full of energy. He could feel life throbbing inside him and a million ideas swirling around in his head. He had overcome the sadness caused by the family's misfortunes, and he abandoned himself to life as it smiled upon him. His neighbors would later say that they could sometimes hear him singing when he was in the house or hurrying out for theater rehearsals.

His academic commitment was also solid. His grades constantly put him at the head of the class, but he was not an ivory-tower scholar—sad and alone, closed in on himself and hunched over his books. One of his professors said one day that among all his students, Karol came closest to being a genius.

He was a young man with a profound commitment to life and a deep desire to have fun, to do things, to play and to sing. He was able to communicate with all kinds of people immediately after first meeting them.

On the youth soccer team he was so good at being a goalie that people called him "Martyna," the name of a popular soccer player of the day. He hiked up the mountains and swam like a fish in the Skawa River.

Dancing was very popular at the time. The grand Austro-Hungarian tradition, with its love for classical music, Strauss waltzes, mazurkas, Polonaises and the popular dances from dance halls had spread to Poland.

Karol had taken lessons to learn the traditional ritual ceremonies: how to invite a girl to dance, how to hold her while dancing, how to lead her back to her seat and then bow. He really liked the atmosphere of formal ceremony, and he became a very elegant dancer. He attended dances at clubs and in private homes and was as successful in this arena as he had been in the theater. Known for being cultured, intelligent and charming—and having an attractive physique—he was considered the king at these gatherings, and everybody invited him to their parties.

Principles and Purity

This seemingly innocent, pleasant and charming state of affairs actually concealed real dangers, especially in light of the mission that was mysteriously entrusted to Wojtyla even before his birth. Karol's striking physical appearance was clearly noticed by the girls his age. Stories corroborate the fact that during these high school years he was the most admired and sought-after young man.

The young men and women of Wadowice spent time with each other at parties—drinking, smoking and flirting. People fell in love and became engaged. There was a place called "Lovers' Lane" where young men would take their girlfriends at night to express their affection in scandalous ways. Even family get-togethers and school trips were opportunities to flirt.

There were, of course, young men and women who chose to be chaste and to deny themselves sexual pleasure for religious reasons. Some of them wanted to become priests or to enter religious life. These young people stayed away from the parties and the outings.

Karol Wojtyla had been raised with strict religious morals and deeply felt religious convictions. However, he was not the kind of person to stay shut up at home away from his friends. He was not thinking of priesthood at this time. His dream was to become an actor, a playwright and a director and to write poetry. He enjoyed parties, entertainment and dancing, and he was not blind to the appeal of young women. He was, therefore, exposed to temptation.

Lolek, however, succeeded in maintaining a consistent inner balance by keeping his passion for theater and his joy in life within the proscribed boundaries of religious and moral principles that he had been taught and that were at the core of his philosophy of life. Even at this young age Karol knew that every young woman is a person, a daughter of God, an immortal being. He knew that there is no greater love toward a young girl than respect. These are solid principles that Wojtyla has communicated through his teaching, his books and, as pope, his wonderful addresses to crowds of young people during World Youth Days.

When Karol Wojtyla was elected pope in October 1978, reporters dug into his private life, particularly his life as a youth. Photographs of young men and women in the mountains—showing Wojtyla dressed in shorts and short-sleeved shirts—began to circulate. Those kinds of photos of an ecclesiastic were absolutely unthinkable at that time in Italy. They sold like hot cakes. Feature magazines began to hoard them, while newspapers used the most respectable ones. In a few days the mountain of photos disappeared. From then on people had to pay millions of the old liras for them.

The reporters sought out people he had spent time with and the people involved in his theater groups. Everyone wanted to find the old girlfriends. There were two young women in particular who seemed close to him during that time, Ginka Beer and Halina Królikiewicz.

Ginka was two years older than Karol and a very talented actress. She lived on the floor above the Wojtyla apartment. She was a very beautiful Jewish girl with striking dark eyes and ebony-black hair. His friends from that period, like Jerzy Kluger, say that Karol always showed up with her at rehearsals and would do all kinds of favors for her, like wax her skis. They saw this as a sign that he was in love with her. Before the Nazi occupation of Poland, however, Ginka's family decided to move away. Karol suffered a lot in losing this companion.

After Ginka left, Karol Wojtyla's attention focused on Halina Królikiewicz. She was also very beautiful and very talented, so much so that she later became a famous professional actress. She was the daughter of the principal of the girls' high school. She and Karol were the two best young actors in Wadowice. Their friendship evolved little by little to the point that some people suspected they were engaged during the war years, when they both lived in Kraków.

There was even a rumor about a phantom wife. Supposedly Wojtyla had married in Kraków in the early 1940s. His wife was then arrested by the Nazis and taken to Germany, where she died in a concentration camp.

Actually, people are not scandalized when they hear these kinds of stories. It would have dealt with a time in Karol Wojtyla's life when he was not a priest and when he wanted to become a great actor. In fact, upon hearing these stories, many people—and especially those who claimed to be indifferent to religion and to the Church—expressed positive reactions. "Finally, someone who has had life experience," they said. "This pope will certainly be able to understand the problems of sex, marriage, family and clerical celibacy."

Believers also accepted this story. In the Church's history there are many examples of men who had a normal, even dissolute, youth who became extraordinary saints. Having a pope who was a fascinating young man of the world seemed perhaps even a good thing.

THE POPE SPEAKS UP

As the days passed, however, the investigation into young Wojtyla's girlfriends and the phantom wife never turned up anything solid. Reporters tracked down Ginka and Helena and mercilessly subjected them to interviews. They both said that Karol was a wonderful young man whom all the young women fell in love with and that he was a unique person.

"Of course, the two women don't want to talk," cynical reporters commented. "It's obvious they don't want to tell the truth and cause scandal. Maybe the Vatican bought them off for their silence."

Curiosity about this issue has never died completely. Every so often some feature magazine has revisited it, adding fanciful specifics, details and insinuations. The Vatican never has intervened.

However, John Paul II believed he should explicitly clarify this aspect of his personal life. In 1996, on the occasion of the fiftieth anniversary of his ordination, he wrote his autobiography, *Gift and Mystery*. He briefly but purposefully touches on the issue of his friendships with women in his youth:

> In that period of my life, *my vocation to the priesthood had not yet matured*, even though many people around me thought that I should enter the seminary. Perhaps some of them thought that if a young person with such evident religious inclinations did not enter the seminary, it had to be a sign that there were other loves or interests involved. Certainly, I knew many girls from school and, involved as I was in the school drama club, I had many opportunities to get together with other young people. But this

was not the issue. At that time I was completely absorbed by a passion for *literature*, especially *dramatic literature*, and for the *theater*.[1]

This was a gentle but clear response to various insinuations and rumors. The issue was clarified also in a letter the pope wrote to Father Wladyslaw Kluz. This Carmelite had written in a biography of Karol Wojtyla that in his youth he had let himself be overcome by temptations of the flesh, that he had had romantic, sexual relationships with some young women, but that he had repented of these sins and was given absolution in confession. The incriminating sentence went something like this: "Confession was the means through which young Wojtyla 'regained' the grace of God."

Perhaps Reverend Kluz was thinking that such a happening would not have been extraordinary or unusual, considering Karol's age and the circumstances. But it was a false conjecture. Because a priest had written the statement and thus it would appear very credible, John Paul II was concerned. The pope wrote directly to the Carmelite monk. Regarding the incriminating sentence quoted above, John Paul II wrote:

To regain implies that I had lost, through a grave sin, the grace of God. Who told you that I committed grave sins in my youth? It never happened. Can't you believe, Father, that a young man can live without committing mortal sin?[2]

These words are valuable in our efforts to get to know Karol Wojtyla. One can tell from his declaration that Our Lady protected him. There are extraordinary "holy sinners" in the Church, but Our Lady wanted this son to be free of any grave sin.

CHAPTER SIX

Entering the Arena ✝

O N MAY 28, 1938, Karol Wojtyla ended his classical studies with flying colors. He had decided without hesitation what he would do with his life: He would immerse himself in the theater as an actor, director and author. Theater had been his passion and would now become his profession. It was a means to express himself as a man and as a Christian. He wanted to prepare in the best way possible, so he decided to move to Kraków to study literature at the Jagiellonian University.

In Poland the last year of high school included preparation for the sacrament of confirmation. In this nation where Christianity was still very alive, confirmation was conferred when young people were able to understand the significance of the sacrament. These young men and women were preparing to enter the arena of life, either to begin studies at a university or to begin a professional career. Many were also thinking about beginning families. The Polish Church chose this time in their lives to confer confirmation, by which they would become "soldiers for Christ."

Karol Wojtyla received the sacrament on May 3, 1938. A few days later the archbishop of Kraków, Adam Stefan Sapieha, visited Wadowice. He was an intelligent, disciplined, charismatic man whom everyone called "the prince." Coming from an aristocratic Polish family, he had friends and acquaintances among all the most important people in Poland. He had worked in the Vatican for several years as secretary to Pius X, who had ordained him as bishop in the Sistine Chapel in 1911.

His visit to Wadowice was one of the normal "pastoral visits" prescribed by the *Code of Canon Law* for those responsible for a diocese. He stopped at the parish, but he wanted to visit the schools because he had a particular interest in young people. When he visited Marcin Wadowita Secondary School, the task of welcoming him fell to Karol Wojtyla. He was the best student in the school and the most well known because of his acting career.

Karol greeted the archbishop with a speech in Latin. The archbishop, who was a very attentive and intuitive person, was struck by the appearance and bearing of the young man. When he asked Father Zacher, the school's religion teacher, for information about him, Father Zacher extolled Karol's intelligence and his spiritual qualities.

The archbishop asked what he planned to do after graduation and Father Zacher said he would enroll at the university in Kraków. *Had Karol thought about the priesthood?* the archbishop wondered. Father Zacher remained silent for a few moments and said that although he would make an extraordinary priest he was completely committed to the theater and planned to be a great actor. The archbishop, disappointed, said that it was a shame he wouldn't be studying theology.

Everyone who knew Karol well was convinced that he would be an excellent priest, but they knew he had chosen the theater. That choice, however, did have a religious motivation. Wojtyla considered the theater a patriotic and spiritual mission, where a person could give testimony to the faith.

AN ACTOR FOR GOD

During his last years at high school, he had become friends with a teacher who was also "smitten"—and very experienced—with theater. Mieczyslas Kotlarczyk was from Wadowice and was nineteen years older than Karol. He had studied literature at the university in Kraków and had graduated with a thesis on theater criticism in the early nineteenth century. He had returned to Wadowice to teach literature, but he dedicated all his free time to the theater that his father was operating in the city. He wrote for publications on national culture, he gave radio addresses, he was current on the latest developments in German theaters, and he was in contact with Juliusz Osterwa, the famous actor-director of the National Theater of Kraków.

Mieczyslas Kotlarczyk was a man of deep faith. He thought of theater as an ascetic, mystical exercise whose purpose was to communicate the Word of God. What counted most in Kotlarczyk's concept of theater was "the Word," *verbum* in Latin, and therefore texts were important. An actor was supposed to become a perfect yet humble instrument to communicate the Word and to be a kind of lay priest serving the Word.

The Word in the theology of St. John the Evangelist is God himself. John's Gospel opens: "In the beginning was the Word, and the Word was with God, and the Word was God." Inspired by John's theological insights, Mieczyslas Kotlarczyk had developed his own theories in that direction and had founded the "Theater of the Living Word."

In his early years of high school Karol began to visit Kotlarczyk's apartment to discuss theater and the importance of language in Polish society. Little by little a genuine friendship between the two developed. It was a friendship that would continue through frequent letters when Karol left Wadowice to study at the university. There young Wojtyla would elaborate on and develop Kotlarczyk's fascinating theories. As pope he would write in *Gift and Mystery*:

> The word, before it is ever spoken on the stage, is already present in human history as a fundamental dimension of man's spiritual experience. Ultimately, the mystery of language brings us back to *the inscrutable mystery of God himself.* As I came to appreciate the power of the word in my literary and linguistic studies, I inevitably drew closer to the mystery of the Word—that Word of which we speak every day in the *Angelus*: "And the Word became flesh and dwelt among us" (Jn 1:14). Later I came to realize that my study of Polish language and letters had prepared the ground for a different kind of interest and study. It had prepared me for an encounter with philosophy and theology.[1]

Wojtyla's encounter with Kotlarczyk was providential. It diverted Karol from a preference for lighthearted entertainment, like singing and dancing, and directed him toward the more serious arts, like theater with social, patriotic or religious content.

LIFE IN KRAKÓW

Karol lived with his father in a house that belonged to relatives at 10 Tyniecka Street. It had been built at the end of World War I. Their apartment was in the basement, while their relatives lived on the floors above.

The house was in a beautiful area full of parks along the Vistula River, but the basement apartment seemed like a wine cellar. There were two bedrooms, a kitchen and a bath. The rooms were dark and damp, and very cold in the winter despite the stove that was always lit. Friends who visited Lolek would call the apartment "the catacombs."

Lolek was used to sacrifices and did not pay attention to the discomforts. Besides, he was generally out for the whole day and often until late at night. The captain had rheumatism, and the humidity caused him pain, but he did not complain.

Karol Jr. immediately fell in love with the city. The stately university, founded in 1634, was one of the most prestigious cultural centers in Europe; Copernicus had studied there. Wawel Hill, the Wawel Castle (the residence of the kings), the cathedral, the Episcopal Palace, the tombs of the saints and kings, Gothic monuments, the medieval squares, the towers, as well as the merchants, the little shops, the cafés, the elegant restaurants, the cultural spots—Karol loved it all and wanted to experience it all.

In addition to his commitment to his studies, Lolek began to make contact with groups of young intellectuals, especially young poets and young actors. In very little time he made significant friendships. He became a member of the "Circle of Scholars of Polish Studies." One of the first young men he became friends with was Juliusz Kydryński, who then introduced him to his other friends, to various clubs and also to a high society family, the Szkockis, who owned a villa on the Vistula River called "Under the Birches."

Every evening there were meetings of poets, artists and musicians at the villa. They discussed literature, philosophy and art and performed concerts and recited poetry. It was a true cultural center, and Karol was immediately welcomed into the family, becoming such a favorite that he called the lady of the house "Grandma."

At the end of his first year of residence in Kraków, Karol Wojtyla was well known. He took part in some performances by an experimental theater group called "Studio 39." The group once performed a play in the courtyard of the university, and many professors attended. Also in the audience was Juliusz Osterwa, the famous actor-director of the National Theater of Kraków, who would later become Wojtyla's friend.

In Kraków Karol contacted Father Kazimierz Figlewicz, who had been his religion teacher and his confessor in 1932 in Wadowice. He found him at Wawel, where the priest oversaw the cathedral, and began to visit him regularly. Every first Friday of the month, he met with him to go to confession, serve Mass and receive Communion. Each time he would linger, spellbound in that place that was the heart not only of faith but also of history and art in Poland.

The Wawel Cathedral is an architectural wonder. It rises on the same hill as the castle, the home of the kings. Inside the castle are the tombs of almost all the kings of Poland. Karol would stop at the very beautiful Sigismund Chapel. He admired the clock tower, which has the most famous Polish church bell, the "Zygmunt." King Sigismund the Elder cast this bell from cannons captured at Wolochy. The church bell rings only during great civil and religious festivals, and when its rich sound fills the sky above Kraków, every citizen feels the thrill. Karol knew the history, the traditions and the people who were evoked by that place because he had met them in the poems and novels he had read since childhood and in the plays he had performed.

PEACE DISRUPTED
Lolek was in Wawel Cathedral on September 1, 1939. He had climbed the hill early in the morning; the cathedral was completely deserted, and he enjoyed the profound silence laden

with memories. As usual, he had attended Mass and received Communion on this first Friday of the month. Then, as he was walking slowly through the half-lit nave, he heard shots. He ran outside.

From the hill he could see the city laid out before him, and in the sky he saw a formation of planes nose-diving to drop bombs. They were aimed at the barracks on Warszawska Street. The sirens were wailing. He heard explosions and shots from anti-aircrart artillery. It was the first aerial attack by the Germans on Kraków.

Karol thought of his father, alone in the basement on Tyniecka Street. He said good-bye to Father Figlewicz and hurried home.

His father was fine. Fortunately the bombs had not dropped on that part of the city. But Karol realized that it was no longer safe to stay in Kraków.

The radio said that the Nazis were invading Poland. The German troops had entered the country and were marching toward Kraków. All the men and boys over the age of fourteen were advised to leave the city and to head east. They were warned not to use trains, which were targets for the German planes.

Karol wasn't sure what to do. He helped his friend Juliusz Kydryński carry some of his family's furnishings out of the city. People were fleeing without any clear destination in mind. German planes were returning frequently to drop more bombs. The radio said that German troops were now at the gates of Kraków.

Karol decided to take his father to a safe place. He packed a few necessary items in a suitcase, and they began walking east. The captain was not well. Living in Kraków in those dark and musty rooms had put a strain on his health. He was an old man before his time. He felt exhausted and walked with great difficulty, leaning on his son.

They were hardly out of the city when they met a truck driver who gave them a ride. They covered a fair distance bouncing along in the vehicle, but then they had to walk again. Every so often they took breaks. Sometimes they had to run away from the road to protect themselves from the machine-gun fire of the German planes. They sought refuge for the night in farmers' houses.

In a couple of days they arrived about 125 miles east of Kraków, only to discover that Russian troops were arriving from the east. They joined the flood of refugees who were forced to go back the way they had come. It was an excruciating march, especially for the captain.

When they returned to Kraków, they found German troops already occupying the city.

The Invasion

For some time Hitler had been thinking of expanding his territory in the east to increase the flow of food supplies to Germany. Now the Nazis had invaded Poland without any declaration of war.

Simultaneously Russia, then allied with Germany, wanted to safeguard its frontiers. There was a nonaggression pact between the two countries. However, Stalin did not trust Hitler and wanted to have a buffer zone between the Soviet Union and the German troops. So sixteen days after Germany invaded Poland, Stalin invaded Poland from the east. The French and English, who were allies with Poland, did not live up to their responsibilities. No one lifted a finger, leaving Poland at the mercy of two unscrupulous madmen.

It was hell for Poland and its thirty-five million inhabitants. By the end of the conflict in 1945, Poland had lost 18 percent of its population. Six million Polish citizens were killed in just six years. Included in the carnage were major massacres of Jews.

The invasion happened very quickly. German troops dropped the first bombs and crossed the borders on September 1, 1939. On September 6 the Germans reached Kraków. On September 17 the Soviet army came across the eastern borders of Poland.

During the night between September 17 and 18, the entire Polish government as well as the cardinal primate of Poland's Catholic Church, Augustyn Hlond, fled the country and escaped to Romania. On September 19 the commander-in-chief of the Polish army also fled the country, leaving the army in disarray.

Warsaw tried to resist, but the Germans cut off the city's water and food supplies, and the city fell on September 27. On October 5 Hitler reviewed the German troops at Warsaw as a symbol of victory.

At the beginning of November the Germans and the Russians divided Poland between them. The Soviets held the region of western Ukraine and Byelorussia up to the Curzon Line—that is, the eastern area of Poland. The Germans incorporated the western and central region into the Reich and instituted a general governorship for the other areas, with Kraków as its capital. Several areas of the country, like Wadowice, were joined to the Third Reich, while the remaining territories were turned into a Nazi colony. A flag with the swastika waved from the top of Wawel Castle, the home of the Polish sovereigns.

Nazi Goals

The command of the general governorship was entrusted to Hans Frank, an ambiguous and contradictory character who fully shared Hitler's ideology of extermination. Frank, a legal practitioner born in 1900, was among the first to join the National Socialist Party and was elected to the Reichstag in 1930. From 1936 to 1939 he was the minister of justice and president of the German Academy of Law.

In his six years as governor Frank sought to eliminate the intellectuals and exterminate the Jewish population. Arrested at the end of the war, he was tried by the International Tribune in Nüremburg and condemned to death. He was hanged on October 16, 1946.

As soon as he arrived in Kraków, Frank let it be known that the Nazis wanted to make Poland disappear. He distributed a kind of *vade mecum* (reference manual) to his collaborators. In harsh, cynical language he explained the philosophy of the occupation and the goals that needed to be reached:

> The Pole has no rights whatsoever. His only obligation is to obey what we tell him. He must be constantly reminded that his duty is to obey.
>
> A major goal of our plan is to finish off as speedily as possible all troublemaking politicians, priests, and leaders who fall into our hands. I openly admit that some thousands of so-called important Poles will have to pay with their lives, but you must not allow sympathy for individual cases to deter you in your duty, which is to ensure that the goals of National Socialism triumph and that the Polish nation is never again able to offer resistance.
>
> Every trace of Polish culture is to be eliminated. Those Poles who seem to have Nordic appearances will be taken to Germany to work in our factories. Children of Nordic appearance will be taken from their parents and raised as German workers. The rest? They will eat little. And in the end they will die out. There will never again be a Poland.[2]

The reign of terror had begun. The smallest infraction of any rule could be punished by immediate death or deportation to concentration camps. The people were supposed to live on nine hundred calories per day.

Secondary and higher education were abolished. Participation in cultural activities was considered a criminal offense. The great Polish Slowacki Theater was renamed "Staatstheater" and was reserved for the Germans. Musical performances of works by Polish composers, including Chopin, were forbidden. Libraries were destroyed, books were burned, and statues of poets and national heroes were smashed.

The Nazis especially hated the Catholic Church, which was prospering in Poland more than in any other European nation. At that time the Polish Church consisted of 5,100 parishes, with 11,300 priests, 17,000 nuns and more than 25,000,000 practicing Catholics. At the end of the Nazi occupation, 3,646 priests had died in concentration camps, and of that number 2,647 had been murdered. There were 1,117 imprisoned nuns, 238 of whom were killed and another 25 who died from hardships and deprivation. In the concentration camp at Dachau alone there were 1,474 Polish priests who had been deported by the Germans.

The Jagiellonian University was closed. On November 6, 1939, the Nazis arrested 184 professors who were part of the faculty of that prestigious university and deported them to the concentration camp at Sachsenhausen-Oranienburg.

There were international protests. Three heads of state—Mussolini in Italy, Franco in Spain and Horthy in Hungary—tried to intervene. They did obtain the release of 120 professors, but the others remained in the camp, most of them eventually dying there. The Nazis looted the university buildings, destroying libraries and laboratories.

CHAPTER SEVEN

The Tailor's School

ACCORDING TO THE REGULATIONS dictated by Hans Frank, every healthy male between the ages of fourteen and sixty was consigned to compulsory labor. Whoever did not work was killed or deported. Lolek quickly found a job as a delivery boy for a restaurant. It was a rather easy job, permitting him time to continue his studies on his own.

But at the beginning of 1940, when the regulations of the Germans became even more rigid, he needed to find a job that was more secure. With the help of friends he became a common laborer at the Solvay chemical factory.

When some writers and lecturers discuss the topic of Karol Wojtyla's work in a factory, they usually speak of it as a temporary job that was somewhat secretive and did not entail a strict schedule or any real sacrifice. Nothing could be further from the truth. Karol Wojtyla started working at Solvay when he was twenty and worked there for four very difficult years.

The first year he worked in a rock quarry, a very deep pit from which limestone was extracted for the production of caustic soda for explosives. Lolek's job was to load the trolleys with the material excavated from the bottom of the pit.

He would walk to the quarry, about a half hour from his house. He wore clothing of thin material and wooden clogs, because there was no money to buy appropriate clothes. In the winter the temperature could go to thirty degrees below zero. Some mornings Lolek had to coat his face with vasoline or bacon fat to prevent it from freezing.

His workday began at dawn and ended at 3:00 P.M., with a fifteen-minute break for lunch around 10:00 A.M. His meager salary was the only income he and his father had, because the captain's pension had been cancelled.

Karol, a tall, strong young man forced to work hard, needed plenty of good nutrition. The Nazis allowed nine hundred calories a day at the most. Lolek thought mostly about his father, who was now old and sick, and gave him most of the nutritious food. Often Lolek's rations consisted of a few potatoes mixed with a bit of onion and a few pieces of stale bread.

Fortunately, after a year, he was transferred from the quarry to a water purification plant at Solvay. The fatigue was constant, the sacrifices were great, hunger was a permanent condition, and his strength was debilitated, but at least now he would be indoors, which would mitigate the effects of winter cold and summer heat. Being on night watch, however, weighed heavily on him because he had to leave his father at home alone.

For four solid years Karol Wojtyla followed this work schedule. That works out to fifteen hundred days, one after another, without a break.

OUR LADY'S CARE

As a boy Lolek had developed a devotion to Our Lady. It has been said that it was his mother who taught him this devotion, and as time went on this devotion grew. Lolek transferred the affection and tenderness he had for his earthly mother to his heavenly Mother.

In high school Lolek had joined the Sodality of Mary, a group of young people committed to encouraging devotion to Our Lady. He had been president of this group for two years in a row.

His devotion to Our Lady was somewhat instinctive but deep. He did not know that Our Lady had spoken about him to the three children at Fatima before he was born. One can imagine that she watched over his growth and formation with a special interest. Once the secret of Fatima was revealed and—after the 1981 attack—the pope recognized himself as the "Bishop dressed in white," he became convinced that the Blessed Virgin had guided his life. In his autobiography, *Gift and Mystery*, he points to his devotion to Our Lady as one source of his priestly vocation and everything that followed:

> Naturally, in speaking of the origins of my priestly vocation, *I cannot overlook its Marian thread*. I learned the traditional devotions to the Mother of God in my family and in my parish at Wadowice. I remember, in the parish church, a side chapel dedicated to Our Lady of Perpetual Help. In the mornings, the secondary school students would make a visit to it before classes began. After classes, in the afternoon, many students would go there to pray to the Blessed Virgin.
>
> Also, on a hilltop in Wadowice, there was a Carmelite monastery that dated back to the time of Saint Raphael Kalinowski. People from Wadowice would go there in great numbers, and this was reflected in the widespread *use of the scapular of Our Lady of Mount Carmel*. I too received the scapular, I think at the age of ten, and I still wear it. People also went to the Carmelites for confession. And so, both in the parish church and

in the Carmelite monastery church, my devotion to Mary took-
shape from the years of my early childhood and adolescence up
through secondary school.[1]

The move to Kraków, university life, contact with young people of that great city, the war and other preoccupations could
have, in a sense, cooled this devotion to Mary. Instead these
things deepened it.

Returning to Kraków, Lolek began to attend the church in
his area, the church of St. Stanislaw Kostka, run by the Salesian
Fathers. As was his custom in Wadowice, every morning Lolek
would make a visit to the church and remain a long while
kneeling in prayer.

THE LIVING ROSARY

This courteous, handsome young man, who prayed with so
much concentration, was noticed not only by the priests but
by a strange, mysterious layperson, Jan Tyranowski. He was a
thin, stoop-shouldered, clumsy man with graying hair
combed back and a high-pitched, almost feminine voice.
Some people thought he was a little crazy. The priests of the
parish did not pay much attention to him. However, Jan
Tyranowski had an enlightened soul, and young Wojtyla
immediately intuited that.

> [T]here was one person who stood out from the others: I am
> speaking of *Jan Tyranowski*. By profession he was a clerk,
> although he had chosen to work in his father's tailor shop. He said
> that working as a tailor made it easier for him to develop his inte-
> rior life. He was a man of especially deep spirituality.[2]

After the invasion the Polish Church was hard pressed. The
Nazis arrested many priests. Of the eight Salesians who
worked at St. Stanislaw, seven ended up in a concentration

camp. In order to keep the faith alive in the parish, especially among young people, the priest sought the help of laypeople. He turned to Jan Tyranowski.

The strange tailor had already taken spiritual initiative with the youth, leading something called the "Living Rosary." At various times he had spoken with the clerics of the parish about this activity, but they had not been interested. Now his work became suddenly important to them, and he was asked to devote himself to it.

The Living Rosary was a Marian initiative aimed at making faith concrete. Members committed themselves every day to the teachings that came from prayer, Scripture and other spiritual books. During the German occupation the movement had to go underground, but in doing so it became stronger and more committed. Whoever joined knew the risk.

The members were divided into groups of fifteen; every group had a leader who reported directly to Jan Tyranowski. During the occupation the movement had around sixty members, the youngest of whom was fourteen. The movement had four leaders; Karol Wojtyla was one of them. Jan Tyranowski occasionally met with the whole group at Mass, but he was always available to see whoever needed to talk to him.

Tyranowski was a real spiritual father for these young people, as well as a guide who was greatly respected, loved and followed. His teachings were basic. The youth needed a clear, concrete understanding of the truths of the faith and of how to put them into practice. He encouraged them to do an examination of conscience every day and to keep a daily written schedule to monitor their activities and faithfulness to their principles.

Tyranowski was a charismatic person who communicated enthusiasm. Karol Wojtyla learned certain habits of self-control

and discipline in the spiritual life. In *Gift and Mystery* John
Paul II writes that from him

> I learned the basic methods of self-formation which would later
> be confirmed and developed in the seminary program.
> Tyranowski, whose own spiritual formation was based on the
> writings of Saint John of the Cross and Saint Teresa of Ávila,
> helped me to read their works, something uncommon for a per-
> son my age.[3]

It was, in fact, Tyranowski who encouraged young Wojtyla to
become acquainted with Spanish mysticism and with the
works of St. John of the Cross and St. Teresa of Ávila. These
works would subsequently have a great influence on his spiritual formation and his theological thinking.

TOTUS TUUS

Tyranowski also contributed to the "maturation" of Karol
Wojtyla's devotion to Our Lady. He was the one, during the
war years, to suggest to Lolek that he read the works of the
great French Mariologist St. Louis Maria Grignion de
Montfort, in particular the famous *Treatise*, a work that is still
foundational in the history of Mariology. That reading helped
Wojtyla move from having an instinctive Marian devotion to
having one that was theological, which has continued
throughout his life. Karol Wojtyla's Marian writings,
addresses, exhortations, documents and encyclicals all echo
readings from his past.

John Paul II's pontifical motto, inscribed on his papal coat
of arms, is *Totus tuus* ("All Yours"). He often has referred to
this phrase at the most significant times in his life, such as
after the 1981 attack. It also is inscribed on the wall in the
Vatican Palace under the windows in his study.

The motto has its origin in Kraków. There Tyranowski
introduced an important change in Karol's Marian devotions.

It was a change that John Paul II recorded and highlighted in *Gift and Mystery* when he noted that he found St. Louis Marie Grignion de Montfort's book, *Treatise of True Devotion to the Blessed Virgin,* helpful. At the time Karol was convinced of Mary's role in leading people to Christ, but he was beginning to grasp that Christ also leads people to Mary, his Mother. Karol didn't want to compromise the worship due above all to Christ and so began to question his devotion to Mary lest it become too great. But de Montfort's book answered his questions. He found that Mary does indeed lead us nearer to Christ provided that we "live her mystery in Christ." The pope acknowledged that de Montfort can be difficult to read because of his antiquated style, but he found the author thoroughly rooted in the Trinity and the Incarnation.

> I then came to understand why the Church says the *Angelus* three times a day. I realized how important are the words of that prayer: "The Angel of the Lord declared unto Mary and she conceived of the Holy Spirit. . . . Behold the handmaid of the Lord: be it done unto me according to your word. . . . And the Word became flesh and dwelt among us. . . ." Such powerful words! They express the deepest reality of the greatest event ever to take place in human history.
>
> This is the origin of the motto *Totus tuus.* The phrase comes from Saint Louis Maria Grignion de Montfort. It is an abbreviation of a more complete form of entrustment to the Mother of God which runs like this: *Totus tuus ego sum et omnia mea Tua sunt. Accipio Te in mea omnia. Praebe mihi cor Tuum, Maria* ["I am all yours, and all I have is yours. I welcome you into all my affairs and concerns. Show me your heart, O Mary."][4]

PRAYERFUL RESISTANCE

Karol Wojtyla remained a member of the Living Rosary throughout the war years. Like all Catholic associations, the Living Rosary was prohibited by the Germans. They considered youth groups to be fertile ground for conspiracies. On one occasion the Gestapo burst into Tyranowski's apartment during a meeting. No one knows exactly what the tailor said to prevent the arrest of those present, but he spoke to the Gestapo police for a long time, and they finally left.

Actually, the association was somewhat subversive in the sense that the participants were Polish youth who were devoted to their country. Their aspirations, desires and dreams aimed at a free Poland at any cost. In their discussions they often spoke of how their country could be rebuilt after the Nazi occupation.

Many of them were in contact with members of the Resistance. Sometimes one of the young people would go to the mountains to meet with Resistance groups. Then that individual would return with new ideas and lead a lively discussion about the need for violent resistance against the invaders. Tyranowski's charisma could remove hate from these discussions and restore balanced Christian wisdom in the end.

Karol Wojtyla was on the same wavelength as Tyranowski. His patriotism was keen but guided by the teachings of the gospel. He never endorsed armed resistance or secret sabotage but believed in resistance through culture and especially through prayer. "Prayer is the only weapon that works," he used to tell his friends, adding, "Remember that we have a duty to ask God for strength to endure all this."

His was not a passive religion of quietism, as someone has said. He was on the front lines but unarmed. He could be subjected to violence without retaliating.

He was also a member of Unia, an underground movement of cultural resistance comprised of young Catholics nationwide. The organization had a military component of about twenty thousand men. However, Wojtyla joined only the cultural arm of the group, sharing the ideas that would deeply influence his philosophy. He never participated in any kind of military activity.

This period of underground activity, of cultural resistance, of political and religious discussions and of meetings to pray together at night—as well as his sense of responsibility for the fifteen young people in his Living Rosary group—were all determining factors in Karol Wojtyla's spiritual formation. But so too were the daily reports during those years of subjection to the Nazis. Workers in the factories continued their discussions about their untenable situations; physical exhaustion was aggravated by scarcity of food; there was continuous suffering, humiliation and oppression due to the occupation, with beatings, raids, arrests and immediate executions in the streets.

One day when he was out walking with his father, he saw an elderly Jewish couple being followed by SS soldiers, who were shooting at the unfortunate couple to scare them and make them run. Holding hands, the two of them fled with mouths wide open because they could not breathe; then they fell to the ground dead. The soldiers laughed, but Karol and his father had tears in their eyes.

These situations could make anyone's blood boil and could lead people to revolt. But it was a time to think things over and calmly reflect. Wojtyla's true leader—the trustworthy guide in that hellish bedlam—was Jan Tyranowski, the gentle tailor. He worked hard every day at his profession while, hidden from the eyes of the world, his work as a "spiritual mentor" developed.

At the end of the war, when Karol Wojtyla entered the seminary, Jan Tyranowski became ill. His task was done. Between 1945 and 1946 he was bedridden for almost a year. He probably had some kind of cancer, leading to an arm amputation. He suffered without complaining and even comforted those

who came to see him. He died in March 1947, smiling at his
friends and clutching a crucifix.

Wojtyla could not go to the funeral; he was in Rome studying the Spanish mystics, to whom Jan Tyranowski had introduced him. In a written remembrance of him, he states that
Tyranowski "was one of those unknown saints, hidden amid
the others like a marvelous light at the bottom of life, at a
depth where night usually reigns."[5]

CHAPTER EIGHT

New Pursuits

KAROL WOJTYLA'S ACTIVITY DURING the war was intense. He was involved in several projects, manifesting the innate fervor for altruism that is common in young people. He sacrificed himself without counting the cost.

He had patriotic and spiritual interests, and he was working in a factory, but his true passion was still the theater. He had founded a theater group with some university friends, including Juliusz Kydryński, Tadeusz Kwiatkowski and Danuta Michalowska. They gathered at Karol's home one night a week to recite the classics. These meetings, attended by about thirty other impassioned youth, were dangerous because they were forbidden by the Germans.

The atrocities that Karol saw at work and in the city during the Nazi raids—the beatings, the innocent people gunned down in the street, the humiliation of respected intellectuals, the starvation and the widespread poverty—ripped apart his soul. Yet he could do nothing but pray and wait.

A Creative Outlet

The internal pressure led him to write. At the beginning of the German occupation he began to write plays. His first work, written between November and December 1939, was called *David*. That work is now lost, so we know little of its content. Shortly after, at the beginning of 1940, he wrote *Job*. That play has been performed several times in Poland and was staged in Italy a few years ago by Ugo Pagliai and Carlo Rao. Inspired by the biblical story of Job, it deals with the perpetual suffering of humanity, God and the mystery of Christ's redemptive suffering. In the play Karol included an explanation that provides a key to its reading:

> The things that happened to Job are happening in our day in Poland and in the world. These events are happening during our time of expectation, our time of longing, for the covenant of Christ forged in the sorrow of Poland and of the world.

In the summer of 1940 Wojtyla finished *Jeremiah*, another play inspired by the Bible but set in Poland in the year 1500.

Karol was now in frequent contact with the famous actor-director Juliusz Osterwa, whom the Nazis had prevented from working. Osterwa was the director of the National Theater of Poland and had founded his own theater group, the Reduta Theater, to perform classical Polish dramas for the general public. Since he could not perform now, he tried to get involved with other kinds of theatrical projects. He approached Wojtyla's clandestine group of young actors and attended the performances that were being held at Juliusz Kydryński's home.

Osterwa was enthusiastic about Karol and wanted to get him involved in some of his own projects. In particular he was interested in new translations of masterpieces from all over the world into modern Polish. Karol made an extraordinary contribution to this project with his translation of Sophocles'

Oedipus, in which he demonstrated a perfect mastery of ancient Greek.

ALL ALONE

On Christmas Day 1940 Karol Wojtyla Sr. became ill. The cold, damp basement apartment and poor nutrition had weakened the old captain's body. Lolek was worried, especially because he could not always be at his father's side to help him. Any absence from his factory job could trigger the Nazis' suspicion; they might then discover his theatrical activities, his work in the Living Rosary—all the prohibited activity for which he was risking his life.

Every morning Lolek would get up early, get his father situated and then go to work. On his return he would run to his father's room with his heart in his throat. He was always afraid that something terrible might have happened.

Lolek's friends tried to give him a hand, especially the family of his friend Juliusz Kydryński. Karol would walk back from work with Juliusz and stop at his house. Juliusz' mother always had a meal prepared to bring home to the captain. Every afternoon Maria, Juliusz' sister, would come home with him for a little while to clean the house and warm the captain's food.

February 18, 1941, dawned a very cold day. His father's health seemed to Karol to be getting worse, but the captain assured him that he felt fine. Karol made breakfast, put it beside his father's bed, helped him to eat and then left for work.

He spent the day depressed, thinking of his father. When his shift was over, he went to the Kydryński home for a meal and for some medicine for his father. Then he hurried home with Maria, Juliusz' sister. Maria went to the kitchen, and Karol went to check on his father, whose room was at the end of a dark corridor.

The captain was dead. He had had a cardiac attack when he had tried to get out of bed.

Maria recounts that Lolek immediately burst into tears. Between his sobs and hiccups, he blamed himself for not being there when his father died, just as he had not been able to be with his mother or his brother. The people he loved the most had all left this world without his presence, and for that he felt guilty. He also blamed himself for his father's dying without the last rites of the Church.

After a little while he ran to the church of St. Stanislaw Kostka to ask the priest to come and bless his departed loved one. Maria, meanwhile, had gone home to tell her family. Juliusz went to Lolek's and stayed with him through the night. Lolek knelt before his father's body all night, praying and talking to his friend, pouring out his very deep sorrow.

On February 22 Father Figlewicz celebrated the funeral. The captain was buried in the military section of the Rakowice cemetery. The Kydryński family, seeing Karol overcome by sorrow, invited him to stay with them for a while, and Karol accepted. He was in no hurry to return to the apartment where his father had died, so he stayed with them for five months. He was not quite twenty, and he was completely alone in the world.

Karol was a changed person after his father's death. The lighthearted cheerfulness was gone. His friends often saw him quiet and sad. They tried to get close and have him confide in them, but his soul was impenetrable.

PASSION RENEWED
Lolek did not let himself be overwhelmed by sorrow. He quickly returned to his activities: his work in the factory, his commitment to the Living Rosary and the theater. His days were full, and he often stayed up late at night.

One thing was certain: Karol loved the theater even more now. He was tireless at rehearsals and had higher standards for himself. The actress Haline Królikiewicz would later say, "In each successive performance the way Wojtyla played his part became more ascetical, more profound." The other actress in that theater company, Danuta Michalowska, said, "[His was a] performance full of tension, in which Karol didn't miss a single accent, a single pause that could be exploited to heighten the listener's emotions."[1]

In July 1941 Professor Mieczyslaw Kotlarczyk had to leave Wadowice. It had become too dangerous for an intellectual to be in plain view in a city that had been absorbed into the Reich. He decided to move to Kraków with his wife, Zofia. He asked his friend Wojtyla for help, and Wojtyla offered to put him up at his apartment on Tyniecka Street. Karol took this occasion to leave the Kydryński family and return home.

Kotlarczyk found work in Kraków as a tram driver and next as a clerical worker, but he continued his interest in theater. He became the mentor for the theater company that Karol Wojtyla had founded. He gave an ideological significance to the productions that aimed at building up intellectual resistance in Poland against the invaders.

Theatrical activity, Kotlarczyk thought, should be "a protest against the extermination of the Polish nation's culture on its own soil, a form of underground resistance against Nazi occupation." The group renamed itself the "Rhapsodic Theater."

In December 1941 Kotlarczyk's sister, sixteen-year-old Maria, had to flee Wadowice to avoid deportation to a German concentration camp. She too came to Kraków, crossing the Skawa River at night. The small apartment on Tyniecka Street now had four occupants.

In *Gift and Mystery* John Paul II writes about this period when, because they lived in the same house, he and Kotlarczyk were able to talk about the theater all the time. They even held performances, using limited scenery and props and concentrating primarily on effectively delivering the text.

Wojtyla's home became a school. All the work, from the writing of the texts to their staging, was done in the basement apartment on Tyniecka Street. Themes, dialogues, characters, ideologies and objectives—everything was the fruit of long discussions, which sometimes would last for weeks.

Rehearsals were on Wednesdays and Saturdays, in the chilly kitchen lit by a candle. Performances were in private homes before handpicked acquaintances who had a special interest in literature or were, to some extent, the "initiated."

The young actors would arrive surreptitiously. The fear of a raid by the Nazis was always looming, with the threat of serious punishment and even deportation to concentration camps.

Karol, besides being the prominent actor during the recitations, was the charismatic leader of these young people. Kotlarczyk was the theoretician, the organizer, but Karol was the soul of the group. It seems that this passion helped alleviate his sorrow and his loneliness.

No one could have imagined that during this very sorrowful period he was moving toward some pivotal decisions.

TURNING POINT

The first important production by the Rhapsodic Theater after Mieczslaw Kotlarczyk's arrival in Kraków was the drama *King-Spirit* by Slowacki. It was presented four times, beginning on November 1, 1941. The audience was quite small, since the play was held in a private home in the afternoon so as to end before curfew.

Karol Wojtyla gave a stirring performance as the king, Boleslaw the Bold. In Kraków people were talking about his intense and original interpretation.

This play was followed by many others: *Beniowski,* another work by Slowacki; then *Inni* by Jan Kasprowicz; *The Wyspiański Hour,* an anthology of scenes taken from three of Wyspiański's works; *The Norwid Hour,* another anthologized play; *Pan Tadeusz* by Mickiewicz; and Slowacki's *Samuel Zborowski,* in which Wojtyla played the sixteenth-century Polish nobleman who rebelled against the constituted order of his day.

This was the last play in which Karol Wojtyla participated. At the end of the third performance in April 1943 he definitively abandoned his involvement in drama and his dreams of being an actor. He had discovered another vocation. He said in *Gift and Mystery* that he was deeply impressed by his life in the theater but he had come to recognize that it was not to be his true vocation.

The death of Karol's father had brought up some significant issues. The captain, with his enlightened wisdom, his quiet sweetness and his crystal-clear moral structure, had been a shining example and a solid reference point for Lolek in his infancy and in his adolescence. To have lost him, and to have lost him at such a critical time in the nation's history, had made Karol feel that the world was crashing in on him.

Karol Wojtyla has rarely displayed his personal emotions and his suffering because of the deaths of his loved ones and has written and spoken little about them. The months he spent in the Kydryński home had helped him reflect. During his sleepless nights he reviewed his life from infancy to adulthood. He reflected on his mother's, his brother's and his father's deaths. He reflected on the war, the atrocities and the dangers he had faced. He wondered why he had not ended up in a concentration camp like so many of his friends.

He began to see some "signs" in all the things that had happened to him. He began to think that every person's life is guided and has a unique design and that facts and events are meant to help us know where our true path lies. In *Gift and Mystery* he affirms:

> [M]y priestly vocation took definite shape at the *time of the Second World War,* during the Nazi occupation. Was this a mere coincidence or was there a more profound connection between what was developing within me and external historical events? It is hard to answer such a question. Certainly, in God's plan nothing happens by chance. All I can say is that the tragedy of the war had its effect on my gradual choice of a vocation. It helped me to understand in a new way *the value and importance of a vocation.* In the face of the spread of evil and the atrocities of the war, the meaning of the priesthood and its mission in the world became much clearer to me.[2]

VOCATION DISCOVERED

It is good to quote here a significant portion of the intimate things Wojtyla shared in his autobiography. There is no other document that comes close to telling what he was feeling and thinking at this time:

> The outbreak of the war took me away from my studies and from the University. In that period I also lost my father, the last remaining member of my immediate family. All this brought with it, objectively, a *progressive detachment* from my earlier plans; in a way it was like being uprooted from the soil in which, up till that moment, my humanity had grown.
>
> But the process was not merely negative. At the same time a light was beginning to shine ever more brightly in the back of my mind: *the Lord wants me to become a priest.* One day I saw this with great clarity: it was like an interior illumination which brought with it the joy and certainty of a new vocation and this awareness filled me with great inner peace.

All this happened against the backdrop of the terrible events taking place all around me in Cracow, Poland, Europe and the world. I experienced directly only a small part of what my fellow countrymen experienced from 1939 onwards. I think especially of my classmates in Wadowice, close friends, some of whom were Jews....

I was spared much of the immense and horrible drama of the Second World War. I could have been arrested any day, at home, in the stone quarry, in the plant, and taken away to a concentration camp. Sometimes I would ask myself: so many young people of my own age are losing their lives, *why not me?* Today I know that it was not mere chance. Amid the overwhelming evil of the war, everything in my own personal life was tending towards the good of my vocation.[3]

When he was fully convinced that he had a vocation to the priesthood, Karol told his friends that he was leaving the Rhapsodic Theater. Everyone was astonished. They knew he was very religious and went to church often, but they also knew that his enthusiasm and interest were focused on art: poetry, literature and theater.

Kotlarczyk was the most opposed. He too was a believing, practicing Catholic, but he was convinced that Karol's vocation was theater—a religious and social vocation that would allow him to bring a great contribution to his country. For one whole evening Kotlarczyk and Karol's other friends tried to convince him to change his mind, but they did not succeed. His decision was irrevocable.

BROTHER ALBERT

In addition to the war, his factory experiences and his father's death, there is one more important factor in Wojtyla's progression toward the priesthood: his "encounter" with a historical personality, whom he came to know intimately at that time from reading his biography. Brother Albert was a Polish

monk who lived in the nineteenth century and has recently
been canonized.

John Paul II said in *Gift and Mystery* that at the height of
his enthusiasm for the theater, he also found himself very
impressed by Brother St. Albert, well known to all Poles. Born
Adam Chmielowski, he was a talented artist and a deeply
courageous man who turned his back on a career in the arts
when he felt that God was calling him to more important
work. *Did St. Albert have some part to play in his own vocation?*
the pope wondered.

Born in 1848, Adam Chmielowski was orphaned as a baby
and was raised by relatives. After elementary school he
attended an agrarian school for two years, and in 1863, when
he was only seventeen, he took part in the uprising against
Russian domination. He was wounded in battle and had to
have his left leg amputated. After the uprising had been put
down, he attended the art institute in Warsaw and then studied painting in Paris and Munich.

Chmielowski became an esteemed artist. He had his first
exhibition in Kraków in 1870. For ten years he continued to
achieve success, but his life was not completely fulfilling.

In 1880 he entered the Jesuit order, but after only six
months, intense exhaustion forced him to return to the world.
Four years later in Kraków, continually driven by the inner
dissatisfaction that was prodding him, he became interested
in the poor and especially the homeless.

This was his call. In 1887, wearing a simple habit, he took
the name "Brother Albert." One year later he made his vows
before Cardinal Albin Dunajewski, who had also participated
in the 1884 revolt against Russia. He then founded the
Albertine Franciscans and, a few years later, the Albertine
Sisters. Living in radical poverty, he dedicated the rest of

his life to the poor and the homeless. He died on Christmas Day in 1916.

John Paul II acknowledges Brother Albert's unique place in the Polish church but emphasized in *Gift and Mystery* that the saint was personally important to him. Brother Albert provided him with an example of someone leaving the arts behind for the sake of God. He also felt that Brother Albert gave him inner spiritual support to make the decision himself and to pursue the priesthood.

Brother Albert mirrored not only Wojtyla's passion for art but also his love for the poor and for spiritual values. He never forgot him, and the pope has said that one of his greatest joys was to preside over Brother Albert's beatification in Poland in 1983 and his canonization in Rome in 1989. Years before, as a young priest, the pope even wrote a play about him entitled *The Brother of Our God*.

Lessons from Theater

Karol Wojtyla never forgot what he had learned in the theater: the ability to communicate through word and action. As priest, bishop, cardinal and pope, his manner of conveying information and transmitting ideas has always had the elegance, the clarity and the impact of a great actor. Even now that he is old and suffering from illness and its pains, he rises to greatness on every occasion.

His physical schedule can be grueling. At times he is before crowds for six or seven hours of religious ceremony, always under the camera's eye. Despite his illness and his tremors, only in rare cases has he cancelled scheduled international trips.

Some of the most spectacular world events in which he was the undisputed protagonist were those of the Great Jubilee in

2000: the bold celebration for the martyrs of the twentieth century at the Coliseum on May 6; the beatification ceremony for Francisco and Jacinta at Fatima on May 13; and his meeting with two million young people in Tor Vergata in August. Each event was vital and alive, basic but powerful—certainly conceived and imagined by a poet, a man of the theater. This is what Karol Wojtyla continues to be.

CHAPTER NINE

Training for the Priesthood ✝

"At its deepest level, every vocation to the priesthood is *a great mystery*; it is a gift which infinitely transcends the individual," says John Paul II.[1] When he found himself catapulted into this mystery, he had no hesitation in changing his life. One morning in the fall of 1942, taking advantage of some free time because he was working the night shift that week, he walked to the residence of the archbishop of Kraków and asked to speak with His Excellency Adam Sapieha. The priest who welcomed him gently asked him why he wanted to meet with the archbishop.

"I want to become a priest," said Karol Wojtyla.

The priest smiled. He was Jan Piwowarczyk, the rector of the seminary. They spoke for a long time, and Wojtyla told him everything about his life.

Father Piwowarczyk already knew a lot about him, his activities and his faith. At the end of their conversation, he took him to the archbishop, and Karol was officially welcomed into the seminary.

However, to tell the truth, it was a seminary that "did not exist."

STUDYING UNDERGROUND

Immediately after the German occupation, the Gestapo had wanted to take control of the seminary in Kraków and downgrade it to a "professional clerical school." The Nazi goal in Poland was to destroy everything, especially the Catholic Church. Corrupting the seminary—which was part of the prestigious Jagiellonian University—meant discrediting the Polish Church.

But Archbishop Sapieha had withstood the Nazis. His courage, moral fortitude and authority were able to withstand even the fierce efforts of Hans Frank, the director of the general governorship. The Nazi government continued to legislate measures, but the archbishop always found a way around the obstacles.

At one point the Germans forbade the admission of new seminarians under penalty of execution by a firing squad. The archbishop, to save the life of his young men, was forced to comply, but he did so only in part. He sent the youngest seminarians back home but kept the theology students on as "parish secretaries," stationing them in parishes around the city. Every so often they would gather at the archbishop's residence for classes.

One day, however, the Nazis laid a trap for these young men and arrested five of them; they were immediately shot. To avoid any other tragedies, the archbishop decided that the seminary would go completely underground. Candidates would continue to live at home, doing their normal jobs, without telling anyone about their new status. They would study during their free time and every so often meet with professors to take their exams.

Karol Wojtyla was one of the first ten students of this underground seminary. The rector gave him some philosophy and theology books. From that point on he asked for the night shift at the factory. He would dedicate himself to study.

Externally everything looked the same. Karol dressed in bourgeois style, went to the factory, spent time with friends and continued his activity with the Living Rosary. His friends at the factory, however, realized that something had changed. They saw him praying more frequently than before and reading big books written in Latin. His generosity to the poor became legendary. One day he arrived at the factory blue from the cold: He had given his jacket to a vagrant on the street.

His fellow workers teased him good-naturedly, calling him "the little priest." But they liked him very much and tried to help him, doing some of his work so that he could spend more time with his books. The women who were in charge of the kitchen would give him bigger pieces of bread when they could, because they knew he was a good young man.

One of his work companions, Józef Krasuski, recounts that Irka Dabrowska, the eighteen-year-old daughter of one of the managers at Solvay and a worker in the cafeteria, was hopelessly in love with Karol. She invited him to her birthday party, but Karol said he could not go. Józef prodded him, telling him of her interest. He told Karol to go there to make her happy and to have a nice meal for a change.

In the end Karol accepted, but perhaps to discourage the young woman, he went to her party in his overalls and wooden clogs. "These are my clean overalls," he said. "The ones I keep for big occasions."[2] Irka was a bit annoyed but continued to pursue him.

SAVED TWICE

Every day before going home to his apartment, Karol went to the cemetery to pray at his father's tomb. In the morning he often went to Archbishop Sapieha's residence to help serve Mass, and the archbishop would invite him to stay for breakfast. The archbishop liked talking to the young man, and as he got to know him he sensed a magnanimous spirit in him. The archbishop began to make plans for Wojtyla.

On February 29, 1944, something happened that could have brought this whole story to an end. It was 3:00 P.M. Karol had finished his shift at Solvay and was heading toward the cemetery. The street was full of German military trucks and vehicles. A division of soldiers was being transferred to another part of the city.

Karol was walking cautiously along the side of the road. Every so often he looked behind him to see if the long column of vehicles had an end, but the procession, making a deafening noise and causing nauseating fumes, seemed to go on forever.

At a bend in the road, a truck skidded to the right and hit Karol Wojtyla full force, hurling him into the ditch. The truck driver certainly saw the man being thrown up in the air, but he did not stop. Every day some Polish person would be killed by a military vehicle, but Polish people were expendable. The truck went on its way, and the column continued to wind its way down the street.

Fortunately, a woman who lived nearby happened to be standing at a window upstairs. She ran down and found the young man in the weeds, bleeding and unconscious. She started shouting at the military vehicles that were still going by and succeeded at getting a German official to stop. Moved by the lady's request, he stopped a truck and ordered it to take the injured man to a nearby hospital.

Karol had a concussion as well as other injuries. He was in a coma for two days, was treated in the hospital for two weeks and then had a month of convalescence. If that woman had not seen him and had not had the courage to get help for him, the world would never have known Pope John Paul II.

Six months later Karol was rescued from another attack by the "forces of adversity." On August 1, 1944, there was an insurrection in Warsaw. The secret Polish army, with the help of the people, tried to liberate the city from the Nazi troops. The Resistance fighters expected the help of the Russians and of other nations, but none of them lifted a finger. Warsaw struggled for a month and then, by Hitler's order, was leveled to the ground.

In the days following the insurrection, the Germans feared that Warsaw's example would be imitated by other cities. To deflect that danger they organized cruel reprisals, massive raids and mass deportation.

On August 6 the reprisal was launched in Kraków. It was the Feast of the Transfiguration, but the day became known in Kraków as "Black Sunday." The Gestapo searched through all apartments. They arrested eight thousand men and boys, many of whom were sent to concentration camps, never to return.

Wojtyla, in his apartment on Tyniecka Street, could hear the shouts of people being arrested and the footsteps of German soldiers on the stairs of his building and in the room above him. He was kneeling on the floor, praying. No one knows why, but the German soldiers did not see the door to his apartment. They continued passing in front of that entrance without trying to enter.

Wojtyla knelt for many hours, even after the soldiers had gone. He prayed in thanksgiving to God for protecting him.

He knew that if they had found him, he would never have been able to become a priest.

SEMINARY LIFE

The next day the archbishop told his trusted aides to notify the ten underground seminarians that they should come see him. The situation was extremely dangerous, and he did not want them risking their lives. The young men arrived at the palace with some difficulty, as the streets were under surveillance by the Gestapo guards.

The archbishop told them, "It is too dangerous for you to live in the city. From now on you'll be staying with me." He gave them old cassocks and procured false documents for each of them. In case of a German search, they should declare they were priests.

Every morning two Gestapo officials went to Solvay to check which factory workers were present. They noticed that Karol Wojtyla's signature no longer appeared, so they reported that to their commander. An investigation was ordered. Guards knocked at the apartment on Tyniecka Street and interrogated neighbors. The incident risked bringing the Gestapo guards to the episcopal palace. That had to be prevented.

Father Figlewicz, in continual contact with Germans, was charged with resolving the problem. He met with the director of Solvay, but the case was already in the hands of the secret German police. Karol Wojtyla was again in grave danger. Father Figlewicz had recourse to his secret contacts in the Gestapo. All documents, cards, registrations and arrest warrants with the name "Karol Wojtyla" were destroyed. Not one trace of him was left for the Germans; it was as though he had never existed.

The experience of being a seminarian had begun for Karol
Wojtyla. He was already in the third year of theology study,
but he had not ever lived in community like a normal seminarian. Now, for the first time, he felt himself part of the insti-
tutional Church in a seminary that had a rector, Archbishop
Sapieha, a spiritual director and professors. For the first time
he was living with companions, like a religious in a monastery.

He would get up at 6:00 A.M., meditate, attend Mass and
have breakfast. Classes would last until midday. Then there
was lunch, prayer, study, meditation and dinner. Everything
was done according to schedule.

No one could suspect that young seminarians were living in
the archbishop's home. The seminarians could not leave or
even look out the windows, the curtains of which were per-
manently drawn. The young men lived in the basement of the
palace. The rooms were like tombs for the living.

Things went on like this for five months. Then, on January
17, 1945, the Soviet Red Army entered Kraków and forced the
Nazis to leave. Karol Wojtyla was liberated by the communists.
It was his first contact with that atheistic ideology, which he
would then fight for the rest of his life.

One fortunate encounter for Wojtyla was with a soldier
from the Red Army. He was a young man, trained in atheism,
who remembered his grandparents speaking about God when
he was a child. He believed that God probably did not exist,
but he had doubts and wanted to know more.

Karol Wojtyla listened attentively to the soldier and had a
long conversation with him. He wrote in his journal that
night, "During our long talk I learned a great deal about how
God impresses himself on human minds even in conditions
that are systematically negative." [3]

A NEW DIRECTION

At the end of the war all the Polish nationals began to think about reconstruction, but their hopes were disappointed and betrayed. Liberated from the Nazi invasion, Poland ended up being given to the Russian Soviets.

Karol Wojtyla did not take time for political discussions about the Polish nation. He was immersed in his theological studies. He returned to the university to complete his third and fourth years of theology.

He was elected vice president of the Fraternal Assistance Society, which focused on poor students. At the beginning of winter his friend Mieczyslaw Kotlarczyk gave him a nice woolen sweater. He immediately put it on, saying that it fit him well and he finally had something to keep him warm. But two days later he gave it to a tramp on the street.

At the beginning of 1946 Pope Pius XII named Archbishop Adam Sapieha a cardinal, a reward for his courage and loyalty to the Church during the Nazi occupation. In March 1946 he went to Rome to receive his cardinal's hat from the pope. He had worked there for several years as a young priest as secretary to Pius X, by whom he had been ordained a bishop. His return to Rome was a healthy plunge into the past for the aging cardinal. He returned to Poland invigorated and full of ideas.

He decided that some of his young priests, especially the most gifted, should go to the Eternal City for at least two years to breathe in the universal atmosphere that reigned in that capital of Christianity. Karol Wojtyla, who was then both a student and an assistant instructor in theology courses at the Jagiellonian University, would be the first.

Wojtyla, however, told the cardinal that he was perhaps not the right person for this assignment. He still wanted to be a priest, but he felt that perhaps he was called to live out his mission through prayer and contemplation rather than through active involvement in the world. He felt himself persistently called to the cloistered life of a Discalced Carmelite.

The cardinal listened in silence, his face unmoved, as Wojtyla bared his soul. Karol said that even before deciding to become a priest he had read the works of St. John of the Cross and St. Teresa of Ávila: *The Ascent of Mount Carmel, The Dark Night of the Soul, The Spiritual Canticle, The Living Flame of Love* and other mystical classics of the sixteenth century. He had continued to reflect on and reread these works. Encouraged by his theology professors, he was now in the process of writing a book on St. John of the Cross and had even begun studying Spanish so that he could read the great mystics' works in the original. "I think I am called to live in a Carmelite monastery," said Wojtyla, concluding his long confession.

Cardinal Sapieha continued to observe the young seminarian in silence. Then, in a very decided manner, he said tersely, "You first need to finish what you began. You will prepare for priesthood and then go to Rome to finish your theology studies."

Karol Wojtyla had learned from St. John of the Cross that one of the foundational steps in spiritual life was obedience to one's superiors. The superior's voice is the voice of God. He made peace with the cardinal's decision. It was good that he had shared his aspirations with the cardinal, but now it was time to obey.

A Priest Forever

In July Wojtyla took his final exams. His grades were excellent, as always. Of his twenty-six exams he received "excellent" in nineteen, "very good" in six, and "good" in one— psychology. Cardinal Sapieha said Karol needed to move up the time of his priestly ordination so that he could begin the academic year in Rome in the fall of 1946. On October 13, after a six-day retreat, Karol Wojtyla was ordained a subdeacon; on October 20, a deacon; and on November 1, All Saints' Day, a priest. The cardinal officiated at the solemn ceremony in his private chapel at the episcopal palace. Wojtyla was the only seminarian ordained that day. A few friends and relatives attended, including Maria Wiadrowska, his mother's sister and his godmother.

Since November 2 commemorates the memory of departed souls, and each priest is allowed to celebrate three Masses, Wojtyla was able to say three "first Masses." He celebrated them at the crypt of St. Leonard in the Wawel Cathedral, offering them for his beloved mother, brother and father.

In the following days he celebrated Mass in the parish of St. Stanislaw in Wadowice and in the Wawel Cathedral. On November 11 he officiated at his first baptism, for a baby girl named Monika, the daughter of two friends from the Rhapsodic Theater: Halina Królikiewicz, the actress with whom he had often shared the stage, and Tadeusz Kwiatkowski.

CHAPTER TEN

The Young Priest

ON NOVEMBER 15, 1946, Father Karol Wojtyla boarded the train for Rome. It was the first time he was leaving Poland.

The train crossed through Czechoslovakia, Germany and France. There were long stopovers in Prague, Nüremburg and Strasbourg. Wojtyla stayed in Paris for a few days as a guest of the Polish seminary there.

He observed everything in his long travels. Even when he was not able to leave the train, his mind assimilated information, sensations and emotions just by observing the countryside, the buildings, the people, their clothes, their mannerisms and their voices. He often consulted the small tourist guidebook that he had brought along.

He arrived in Rome at the end of November. He obtained lodgings with the Pallottine Fathers until he could move into the Belgian College, a residence for seminarians that Cardinal Sapieha had chosen for his time in the Eternal City.

Roman Guest

Post-war Rome was not a comfortable or rich city. At the Belgian College the rooms were stark—cold in the winter and hot in the summer—and the food was neither plentiful nor good. As always, Karol Wojtyla did not seem to notice these discomforts.

On the contrary, he was quite taken with the enduring beauty and appeal of Rome. He traveled through the city to view artistic masterpieces and to learn about Rome's cultural and historical heritage. Here were the memories of early Christianity, the history of the martyrs whom he had read about since childhood in *Quo Vadis?*.

Every Sunday he went to St. Peter's, where he felt the heart-beat of Christianity. He would stop to look at the tourists who came from all over the world. He would wait for hours to see the pope come to the basilica for liturgical celebrations.

Rome gave him an intoxicating, global overview. There were priests and seminarians from many nations at the Belgian College. At the Angelicum, the pontifical university he attended, there were professors of the highest caliber from many European nations and even from America. Listening to them, watching them and conversing with them, he absorbed new ideas, experiences, aspirations and cultures.

He took this opportunity to perfect his French and German, which he had studied with his father, as well as the Spanish he had learned on his own. He also began to study English and Italian.

He was interested in new theological trends but also in a variety of pastoral experiments, especially those coming from France, Belgium and Holland, like the Priest-Worker Movement and the Young Christian Workers Movement. He had an opportunity to meet the founders and representatives of those movements, and he continued to stay in contact with them in later years.

When he had free days during Christmas, Easter and summer vacations, he took trips around Italy to visit historical sites.

PADRE PIO

Karol's chief academic interest continued to be mystical theology. In fact, he had chosen as the topic for his thesis *The Doctrine of Faith in St. John of the Cross*.

He knew that in Apulia there was a Capuchin monk who, since 1918, had borne the marks of Christ's passion. Some clerics admired Padre Pio; others, citing the opinion of Father Agostino Gemelli, the founder of the Italian Catholic University, believed that Padre Pio's stigmata was the result of hysteria.

Karol Wojtyla heard the opinions and weighed their merits, but he wanted to see for himself. He felt an instinctive attraction to this man. He and some friends organized a trip to San Giovanni Rotondo during Easter vacation in 1947.

Not much is known about this first visit with Padre Pio, but suffice it to say that it was important. Wojtyla stayed at San Giovanni Rotondo for almost a week. This was an opportunity to meet Padre Pio, talk to him, observe him and confess to him.

I have written about ten books on Padre Pio. Almost all of the dozens of people I have interviewed about him have told me that he had the gift of reading people's hearts and seeing the future. In face-to-face meetings he would reveal details about a person's life that would later be fulfilled to the letter. Biographies on Padre Pio are full of stories about his charismatic gift, and some of these incidents were recounted during the rites for his canonization.

The question naturally arises, what revelation did Padre Pio give Karol Wojtyla in 1947? We don't know any specific details. However, when Wojtyla was elected pope, one news agency discovered that in 1947 the young priest Karol Wojtyla had visited San Giovanni Rotondo. The story that Padre Pio had predicted his papacy at that time was picked up by newspapers throughout the world.

When the assassination attempt occurred in St. Peter's Square three years later, that same news agency rereleased the 1947 prophecy by Padre Pio. It also reported that Padre Pio had told Karol Wojtyla, "I see you in a white robe, and that robe is stained with blood." This item too was picked up by the international press.

These stories are probably urban legends. Nevertheless, I clearly remember that they seemed to have a certain credibility at the time of the papal election. A Polish monsignor who knew Wojtyla well told me that when Karol Wojtyla was a young priest and a professor at Lublin University, he liked to joke about this topic, especially with his friends. When they would praise him for his books or other endeavors, he would laughingly respond that a saint had predicted that he would one day be pope. He thought it was ridiculous and impossible.

After he became a bishop he avoided references to that prophecy, and after his election as a cardinal he never spoke of it again.

These details cannot be precisely confirmed. However, one thing is certain: Karol Wojtyla retuned from his visit with Padre Pio tremendously impressed. He was convinced that this holy man was truly "marked" by God, a true saint. He would later have recourse to him and be granted a wonderful miracle.

It is well known that after Padre Pio's death, Wojtyla, who was by then a cardinal, was among the first to move forward the cause of beatification for this "monk with the stigmata." Later, when his cause encountered serious obstacles, Wojtyla, then Pope John Paul II, personally intervened to move it ahead. If it had not been for him, the beatification of Padre Pio would probably still be pending.

A TRUE CONTEMPLATIVE

During his summer vacation in 1947, Karol Wojtyla went to Paris, Belgium and Holland. He wanted to get to know the different avant-garde Catholic social movements that he had heard about in Rome. For one month he was the chaplain for a community of Polish miners in Belgium. He went down in the mines, and he visited miner families. It was a unique pastoral experience.

Returning to Rome, he finished his thesis on St. John of the Cross. On June 14, 1948, he took his exams for the doctorate. He defended his thesis on June 19 and received the highest grade possible, but the Angelicum required a student to publish his thesis in order to obtain the doctorate. Wojtyla did not have the money for that kind of expenditure, so he left without the title of "Doctor." When he returned home, he submitted his thesis to the theology department at the Jagiellonian University. He received the title "Doctor of Sacred Theology" in December 1948.

During his two years in Rome, Karol Wojtyla met scholars of international renown and proved he had uncommon intellectual gifts that would allow him to undertake a scholarly career. However, he also had many new pastoral experiences and others that were more strictly mystical. Returning home, he would certainly have evaluated those experiences, especially in light of the future. What would he like to see develop in Poland?

He was aware that he was gifted intellectually and pastorally, but he still felt a very strong call to the contemplative and monastic life. Once more he went to Cardinal Sapieha and asked permission to enter the Carmelite order. And once more the cardinal answered with a terse "no." But this time young Wojtyla's convictions were quite strong. He thought perhaps the cardinal had not quite understood or had misjudged his desire. It was not a whim or fancy; he definitely felt called to contemplative life.

Unable to convince the cardinal, the zealous Wojtyla went to the superior of the Carmelites in Poland. This man warmed to Wojtyla's request so much that he went to talk to the cardinal himself. Adam Sapieha listened patiently, but once more the answer was "no." He added in a prophetic tone, "We have only a few priests and Wojtyla is badly needed in the diocese. And later will be needed by the whole Church." [1]

In the course of Church history, there have been popes who began as monks, but the ordinary path to papacy is through the ranks of ecclesiastical hierarchy. Someone becomes a bishop, then a cardinal, and then a pope is chosen by the cardinals. If Wojtyla had been cloistered in a monastery, he might well have become a holy monk, even a saint, but it would have been almost impossible for him to become a pope in the Catholic Church. This desire for the cloister, although holy, could have been a temptation from that enemy who did not want him to fulfill the mission that Mary wanted to bring forth in the world.

Yet once more Karol Wojtyla needed to remember that the voice of one's superior is to be received as the voice of God. He put aside his mystical aspirations. But like all great holy men, he succeeded in combining a life of frenetic activity with a life of intense, monastic prayer.

In the offices of the Russian Secret Service in the former palace of the KGB, there is a huge dossier on John Paul II. According to reports from Russian spies operating around the Vatican in the 1980s, Karol Wojtyla dedicated no less than six hours to daily prayer. His day began at 5:00 A.M. with prayer in the private chapel. There was one hour of meditation to prepare for Mass and then meditation after Mass until 8:30. Throughout the day every free moment was dedicated to prayer. Even in the evening he would go to the private chapel for a long time.

Sometimes the prayer was so intense that his aides could hear him moaning and groaning. At times, if it were very late, they would enter the chapel and find him outstretched on the cold marble floor, motionless, with his arms held out in the form of a cross.

Although he was not allowed the contemplative life in a monastery, he lived in the world and prayed like a true contemplative.

FIRST ASSIGNMENT

Father Karol Wojtyla was assigned an assistant pastorship for the Assumption of Our Lady Church in Niegowić, a small isolated village at the foot of the Carpathian Mountains, about thirty miles from Kraków. The pastor of the parish, Kazimierz Buzala, was a man whom Cardinal Sapieha trusted.

Wojtyla left for this assignment full of emotion. It was his first contact with people for whom he was responsible before God. He decided to dedicate his life to them, and he loved them even before meeting them. His faith brought to mind an insight that moved him deeply: He would be bound to these people not for one, two or ten years but for all eternity.

In *Gift and Mystery*, written in 1996, forty-eight years after his arrival in Niegowić, John Paul II vividly recalled his joy upon receiving the appointment and recounted his journey to the parish, first by bus, then by cart and finally on foot. He took a shortcut through fields of grain half harvested, half waving in the wind, with the church of Niegowić visible in the distance. When he got there, he knelt and kissed the ground, a sign of reverence he learned from St. John Vianney, the Curé of Ars, and then prayed before the Blessed Sacrament before going to greet the pastor.

The new priest, before meeting the pastor, took time to acknowledge Jesus, his real superior, his true companion and the person with whom he wanted to live in constant communion.

Father Karol Wojtyla had a small suitcase, mostly full of books. He wore a threadbare cassock and old, worn-out shoes. He did not have any special dietary needs and had no attachment to worldly possessions.

The Niegowić parish, like the countryside, was rural. There was no electricity, no running water and no indoor plumbing.

Besides saying Mass, Wojtyla's assignment was to teach religion to the students in the five elementary schools in Niegowić and the surrounding areas. Traveling in a horse-drawn cart, he would take long trips through the countryside and meditate. To keep in shape physically, he helped the farmers in the fields. He spent many hours in church, kneeling before the altar.

The inhabitants of Niegowić were surprised that Father Karol Wojtyla lived alongside them in their own simple way. They gave him a lovely pillow and a new quilt, and he in turn gave these items to an elderly lady who had been robbed. He often slept stretched out on the bare floor.

He had not forgotten any of his teenage experiences. He organized a theater group in the parish, helping the young people stage *The Guest*, a play in which he played the role of the guest-mendicant who turns out to be Jesus. He also founded a branch of the Living Rosary.

Wojtyla's presence brought a wave of new life to that rural location. People especially noted that young people were enthusiastically attending parish functions and wanting to get involved. He even found a way to replace the old wooden church building with a new brick one.

CHAPTER ELEVEN

Confronting Communism

AFTER THE WAR THE nations of Eastern Europe were almost all absorbed by the Soviet Union, with its atheistic communism. Eliminating or, at least, blocking the Catholic Church was the order of the day for the communists. In Yugoslavia the bishop of Zagabri was accused of collaborating with the fascists during the war and condemned to sixteen years of hard labor. Cardinal József Mindszenty, the primate of Hungary, was arrested and falsely accused of treason; he was condemned to life imprisonment. In Czechoslovakia Archbishop Josef Beran was condemned to fourteen years in prison. Thousands of priests, monks and nuns were arrested in Czechoslovakia and Hungary.

The communist leaders knew that approach would not be effective in Poland. The Polish people were 95 percent Catholic and had remained faithful to the Church throughout history. The communists decided to use different methods to crush the Polish Church.

Above all, they aimed to secure the loyalty of the youth. For that reason they were not happy about activities like those of Karol Wojtyla in Niegowić. It was irrelevant that Wojtyla was moving in a small circle, because the communists knew he could easily be transferred from Niegowić to Kraków. Father Wojtyla needed to be stopped.

The Polish communist leaders decided to dissolve the Catholic association Wojtyla had formed in Niegowić and replace it with a socialist group. They sent observers to Niegowić with orders to discredit the priest. However, the two people assigned to that job could not find anything of which to accuse him. Wojtyla's behavior with the boys and girls was above reproach.

The observers zeroed in on Stanislaw Wyporek, a young man who had become a kind of secretary for Wojtyla because he could type. They promised him many things if he would betray Father Karol, but Stanislaw absolutely refused. The police arrested him in the street, took him into the country-side and beat him savagely.

"They will end up destroying themselves," Wojtyla said prophetically when he went to the hospital to visit his young friend. This priest would give the communists an exceedingly hard time until they were destroyed.

The communists had favored the formation of the Association of Patriotic Priests. Although this group was a Catholic initiative, it was subject to the state. The communists aimed at shaping public opinion in their favor through this group.

Pretending to safeguard religious liberty, the government promulgated a decree that actually aimed at reinforcing its control over the Church. The decree recognized papal supremacy in matters of ecclesiastical jurisdiction, such as the naming of bishops. It allowed public worship and pilgrimages.

The Church was to be in charge of religious education in state schools, to retain chaplains in hospitals and prisons, to publish independent newspapers and to appoint parish priests and seminary personnel. The government also permitted the Church to continue its activity at Lublin University, the only institution of its kind throughout the entire communist world where Church involvement was allowed. In exchange, the Church was obliged to exhort the faithful to work toward social reconstruction and to discourage any activity that was hostile to the republic.

The Polish Church had accepted the government's offer because refusal meant martyrdom. Rome's opinion was that the Polish Church had made too many concessions. For their part, the hierarchy of the Polish Church believed that with a temporary cessation of hostilities, they could organize and prepare for the struggle.

BACK TO KRAKÓW

The elderly Cardinal Sapieha realized that new leadership needed to be raised up, young laypeople who were solid in their faith and well trained on a cultural level. He chose Karol Wojtyla for this project.

Wojtyla had been in Niegowić for only eight months. The cardinal knew the communists were keeping him under surveillance. He took advantage of the situation to bring Wojtyla back to Kraków and have him mentor the college students who met at the Church of St. Florian.

Cardinal Sapieha's plan was shrewd. The Polish Church would indeed organize and become strong. When the communist government realized what was happening a few years later, it was too late.

Then they proclaimed the separation of church and state: They closed the minor seminaries and disbanded Catholic

associations. They decided that bishops and priests should be
appointed by the state and that priests had to swear an oath of
loyalty to the republic. The bishops, under the leadership of
Primate Wyszyński, resisted. They were arrested, including
Cardinal Wyszyński, but the Polish Church refused to bend.

Karol Wojtyla's activity at St. Florian's was invaluable
for the Polish Church. He was not trained in a seminary
atmosphere and had not assimilated the narrow mindset and
ecclesiastical culture that are often transmitted in those insti-
tutions. He thought like a layperson with a wide-ranging per-
spective. He would analyze a situation objectively and then
develop a plan leading straight to the goal. Some people were
leery of his fresh ideas, but over time they accepted them.

The communists saw men and women who steadfastly
loved their families as a danger to their efforts to dismantle
society and religion. The government controlled the flow of
work and school schedules with the aim of separating parents
from their children as much as possible. The workday began at
6:00 or 7:00 A.M., so preschool children had to be brought to
daycare centers run by the state. Schools were redistricted to
move children out of their local communities. A permissive
abortion law was promulgated to make abortion a means of
birth control.

Wojtyla realized he needed to counter these policies with
activities that would reinforce family ties and constitute strong
reference points based on the moral and spiritual values of
family. The time for pious exhortations was over. The people
needed to be informed about their enemy and, above all, to
understand the underlying foundation of their convictions.

One day some of the young people from Niegowić went to
see Wojtyla at St. Florian's. They saw he had the works
of Marx, Lenin and Stalin on the shelves in his library and

jokingly asked if he had become a communist. When you want to defeat an enemy, he replied, you need to know what he thinks.

RODZINKA

At St. Florian's Karol Wojtyla held classes, lectures, meetings, spiritual retreats and cultural and artistic activities. He set up a choir that sang traditional Polish songs—a link to tradition. The young people were attracted to music, and the choir at St. Florian's was a success.

Knowing that young people like to belong to something, he set up a group that was initially called *Rodzinka* ("little family"). Its name was changed to *Paczka* ("packet" or "parcel") and then to *Srodovinko Wojtyla* ("Wojtyla's Circle").

Karol Wojtyla wanted to educate not only through weekly lectures and meetings but especially through one-on-one conversations and community living. Since it was difficult to accomplish this within the city of Kraków, where the secret police watched everything from every angle, he would take the young people to the mountains periodically.

The pretext was a week of vacation to camp, hike, ski and go kayaking. Far from the eyes and ears of the regime, he was able to speak and act freely. The young people could fully live out their ideals and their faith. Doing all of this in the great outdoors made it even more appealing.

It was forbidden for clergy to set up activities outside the parish. If Wojtyla had been caught, he could have been arrested. Therefore, he wore casual clothes, sometimes shorts and a short-sleeved shirt, to look like one of the group. He made the youth call him "Uncle."

Those who participated in these excursions remember them as wonderful, invigorating, life-changing events. Wojtyla set up a special schedule for the group, which could consist of two or three boys and girls. He would discuss things with them, eat with them and hike with them. He did this all day long so that the issues could be discussed from all angles.

One of the most important topics concerned sexuality. This is a fundamental issue in the formation of young people because it is at the heart of love, marriage and family. The clergy at that time generally avoided dealing with the issue. Whenever they did have to face it, they did so in the old tradition of reticence and false modesty.

Wojtyla, on the other hand, knew that young people needed to understand sexuality thoroughly in all of its physical, emotional and passionate aspects within the context of God's purpose. He believed and taught that marriage was a real vocation like priesthood and that "the sexual drive is a gift from God."

> Man may offer this drive to God exclusively through a vow of virginity. He may offer it to another human being with the knowledge that he is offering it to a *person*. It cannot be an act of chance. On the other side, there is also a human being who must not be hurt, whom one must love. Only a person can love a person. To love means wishing the other's welfare, to offer oneself for the good of the other. When, as a result of giving oneself for the good of another, a new life comes into being, this must be a giving arising out of love. In this area one must not separate love from desire. If we respect desire within love, we will not violate love.[1]

Father Karol Wojtyla spoke a language young people could understand. They were drawn to him because he dealt with issues that were pertinent to their lives. They listened and asked a lot of questions.

ON MARRIAGE

Wojtyla's educational methods and ideas were uncommon for that time, and so they were somewhat suspect. Some years later, when he was a university professor, he collected his ideas and teachings in a book, *Love and Responsibility*. Without apology Wojtyla dealt with topics like sexual passion, women who are unfulfilled in sex, fake orgasms and the need for the husband to ensure that his partner experiences pleasure during intercourse. This book has become a fundamentally important educational text, notwithstanding a lot of criticism from traditional clergy when it was first published.

Wojtyla believed that in marriage man and woman are equal, which was an avant-garde position in those days. He affirmed that "[a] 'marital' sexual relationship outside the framework of marriage is always objectively a wrong done to the woman. Always—even when the woman consents to it, and indeed even when she herself actively desires and seeks it." [2]

He educated the young people about tenderness, without which "the man will only attempt to subject the woman to the demands of his own body, and his own psyche." [3]

> It must be taken into account that it is naturally difficult for the woman to adapt herself to the man in the sexual relationship, that there is a natural unevenness of physical and psychological rhythms, so that there is a need for harmonization, which is impossible without good will, especially on the part of the man, who must carefully observe the reactions of the woman. If a woman does not obtain natural gratification from the sexual act there is a danger that her experience of it will be qualitatively inferior, will not involve her fully as a person. This sort of experience makes nervous reactions only too likely, and may for instance cause secondary sexual frigidity. Frigidity is sometimes the result of an inhibition on the part of the woman herself, or of a lack of involvement which may even at times be her own fault. But it is usually the result of egoism in the man, who failing to recognize the subjective desires of the woman in intercourse, and the objective laws of the sexual process taking place in her, seeks merely his own satisfaction, sometimes quite brutally. [4]

Through his pastoral activity Wojtyla formed a group with a new mindset about life and religion. The group's numbers increased. Some couples married and had children. Wojtyla kept track of them with a genuine fatherly affection. Even when he was a bishop and a cardinal, he found time to visit his "young people," who had now grown up, to listen to their problems and baptize their children. As pope he still held them in special regard.

Those young people, in turn, were like seeds that spread the ideas and the "Wojtyla" style in their workplaces, their families and whatever groups they belonged to later. Even today in Poland there are groups who are still inspired by that initial experience that Karol Wojtyla had called *Rodzinka*.

CHAPTER TWELVE

This Is My Path ✝

O N THE MORNING OF July 23, 1951, the stentorian voice of "Zygmunt," the bell cast from canons at Wolochy by King Sigismund the Elder, was heard over Kraków. Cardinal Adam Stefan Sapieha had forever closed his weary eyes. He was eighty-four. Kraków mourned the old, indomitable prince. He had been the spiritual leader of the Polish people during the resistance against Nazi Germany in World War II.

Karol Wojtyla also wept. Cardinal Sapieha had been like a father to him. The "prince" had, in a sense, become a substitute for the "captain."

An enormous crowd passed before the cardinal's body at Wawel Cathedral. Even the Soviet newspapers commemorated him. The funeral services were stately. The prince's body was laid to rest under the marble pavement in front of the sarcophagus of St. Stanislaw.

Only one person could take the prince's place at this difficult time in the city's history, Bishop Eugeniusz Baziak. He was the bishop whom Sapieha had kept at his side during the last

years of his life. Cardinal Sapieha had let it be known that at
this difficult time Baziak was the right man to oversee the diocese of Kraków. There was no nepotism or human preference
in this choice: It was prophetic guidance for the good of the
country under the communist regime.

Baziak carried the scars of communist persecution. Born in
1890, he had experienced childhood poverty, obstacles to
study and a complicated career. He was nominated archbishop
in the Latin rite in 1945 at Lwów, a city that had a turbulent
history and had seen a veritable slaughter of Jews and
unspeakable violence and cruelty during the war. The Treaty
of Potsdam ceded the city to the Ukraine, part of the Soviet
Union.

Baziak was named archbishop when the city still belonged
to Poland. It was a prestigious appointment because the episcopal seat for this city goes back to 1412. Shortly after his
nomination, when the city passed into the hands of the
Soviets, Baziak was imprisoned, then expelled. At that point
Cardinal Sapieha invited him to Kraków to serve as a personal
aide in overseeing the diocese.

Now the communist government, aware that Baziak had
been condemned by the communist party, vetoed his selection
as archbishop of Kraków. The Church did not give in. Baziak
remained in his position, even though he could not officially
use the title "archbishop of Kraków." The archdiocese of
Kraków, from the juridical-historical point of view, was
"vacated" for twelve years.

The Stalinist pressure on the Polish Church was at its height
at this time. Baziak, supported by the pope but in disfavor
with the government, felt it was his job to resist at all costs and
demonstrate to the enemy that he was intransigent, tough
and inflexible. He was arrested, but that did not intimidate
him. After being freed he governed the Church forcefully

and vigorously, maintaining a rigid stance even with his own aides.

FURTHER STUDIES

Baziak decided that Karol Wojtyla needed to return to academic life, an idea Cardinal Sapieha had suggested. The prince perhaps had wished to see the plan unfold gradually, but the times were becoming more difficult in Poland. Bishop Baziak proposed that Wojtyla earn a second doctorate and publish his thesis. A second degree would open the doors for him to become a university professor.

Wojtyla, however, wanted to continue his pastoral work with young people, as he believed it was very important. Baziak recognized the importance of the work and promised Wojtyla could continue that apostolate if he could reorganize it. But the Polish Church needed him to become a spokesman for the intellectuals. As usual, Baziak ended the conversation with precise instructions: "I give you two years to write and defend a new thesis."

Wojtyla left the parish house at St. Florian's for an apartment in Old Town, the historical part of the city, and began his new life as an intellectual. The topic for his new thesis was *An Assessment of the Possibility of Erecting a Christian Ethic on the Principles of Max Scheler.* Max Scheler (1874-1928), a German philosopher, had dedicated his philosophical research to applying phenomenology to the world of values, seeking to establish an objective hierarchy of values, with material values on the bottom and religious values at the top.

Baziak commissioned Wojtyla to become a philosopher. He had to immerse himself in the study of phenomenology to begin his research on ethics, which led him to become a genuine philosopher. His research was difficult and complicated, but he went at it with his usual wholehearted commitment and obtained his usual extraordinary success. He is now among the most outstanding representatives of our time in the field of phenomenology.

In those years, because he was forced to live the sedentary life of a scholar, Karol Wojtyla began writing poetry and plays again. He published some of these under pseudonyms—Andrzej Jawień and Stanislaw Andrzej Gruda—because he did not want anyone to confuse his work as a priest, philosopher and theologian with his work as a literary author.

This new life, ordered around a strict schedule that he had learned from his father, enabled him to do what he wanted. He continued his educational conversations with groups of young people who had emerged from "Wojtyla's Circle." He dedicated himself to poetry and drama while doing scholarly research, which gave him satisfaction and earned him prestige, despite the challenges.

Teaching

Wojtyla completed his task in the two years Monsignor Baziak had allocated. He had just finished his thesis but not yet defended it when he was invited to teach a course in social ethics in the theology department at Kraków's Jagiellonian University. He began lecturing in October 1953. At the beginning of 1954 he defended his thesis, and Jagiellonian University conferred a second doctorate.

However, before he could be formally made a lecturer, the communist regime disbanded the theology department at the Jagiellonian University. Wojtyla continued his lectures on social ethics at the Institute of Theology near the Kraków Seminary. Simultaneously, he began teaching at the Catholic Lublin University, which was at that time an extraordinary bastion for Catholic culture. It was the only university run by the Catholic Church within the vast territory dominated by atheist communism.

Established in 1918 by a Polish priest, Idzi Radziszewski, Lublin University had a complicated history. Its beginning was, interestingly enough, due to Lenin. After the Revolution in October 1917 and the beginning of the official persecution of every kind of religion in Russia, Lenin closed the Polish Academy of Theology in St. Petersburg. However, he allowed Idzi Radziszewski to transport the library and scientific equipment from that school to Poland.

In 1939 the Nazis closed the university; the professors were deported, tortured and killed. At the end of the war the university reopened, but it was beset by many difficulties because of Stalinist opposition. Somehow the university managed to survive. This was the university from which Stefan Wyszyński, primate of Poland, had graduated in canon law.

These were hard times for the Catholic Church in Poland. The regime arrested priests and bishops. Two priests, friends of Wojtyla, were condemned to death. The chancellor and nine professors at Lublin University were arrested. Primate Wyszyński, who was made a cardinal in January 1953, was arrested the night of September 25 of that year and imprisoned in a former monastery in the northwestern part of Poland and later in a convent in the south.

Teaching at Lublin was dangerous, but Wojtyla was not afraid. During the academic year he went to Lublin every two weeks. To save time he traveled by train at night, using the trip for reading or meditation. He did not take up permanent residence at the university because he wanted to continue his commitments to the young people in Kraków. He slept in one of the rooms that were reserved for visiting professors. Once when no rooms were available, he slept on a table in the kitchen.

His students recalled, after his election as pope, that he wore an old cassock and an equally old overcoat. He would send his stipend to a scholarship foundation that assisted poverty-stricken students. He ate when he could and only a little. He was very popular with the students. In nice weather he liked to hold class outdoors, on a hill or on a mountain path.

Many of his poems from this time period were published in *Znak* ("Sign"), Kraków's monthly magazine, and in *Tygodnik Powszechny* ("Universal Weekly"). He also finished a play he had been working on for some time, *The Brother of Our God*, which was inspired by the life of Brother Albert. Then he wrote *The Jeweler's Shop*, a poetic reflection on the mystery of marriage, inspired by conversations he had with the young people in his group.

Wojtyla was a university professor, educator, writer and poet, but he was also a priest dedicated to administering the sacrament of confession. He was happy with his work and with his lifestyle, free of any attachment to money or to a career. His joyful liberty could be seen in his choice of an elegant burgundy beret, instead of the traditional black ecclesiastical cap, and horn-rimmed glasses. He looked the part of a poet or an artist.

THE PRIMATE'S PEROGATIVE

A university position rarely leads a priest to the papacy. Wojtyla's new professional niche could have distanced him from the destiny that was prophesied. He would need to become part of the ecclesiastical hierarchy if he were ever to become the pope. And the person responsible for naming bishops in Poland did not think highly of him. That man was the Polish primate, Stefan Wyszyński.

Wyszyński had been leading the Polish Church for three years when Sapieha died. He was a great cardinal, destined to hold that assignment for over thirty years. John Paul II later called him the "primate of the century."

Born in 1901, this professor of social science had a patriotic past. During the Nazi invasion he had been part of the resistance movement as a secret chaplain, with the code name "Sister Cecilia." After the war he wanted to return to teaching, but in 1946 Pius XII made him a bishop and, in November 1948, the archbishop of Warsaw and the primate of Poland.

We know that Wyszyński later became one of Wojtyla's closest friends and admirers. It was he who prophetically told him that he would carry the Church into the third millennium. However, in the 1950s Poland's primate did not have a high estimation of Professor Wojtyla. The two probably did not know each other well. Furthermore, Wyszyński was practical, concrete and interested in social problems, while Wojtyla was a theoretician, a philosopher, a poet and a mystic.

In those years of intense hostility between the Polish Church and the communist regime, Wyszyński had been granted full powers by the pope. The communist government took advantage of every opportunity to veto Church proposals and to generate friction and difficulties. They especially interfered with the naming of bishops, hoping to prevent significant people from being at the head of a diocese. Whenever Wyszyński would propose someone, the government would veto him.

To avoid this ping-pong game, Pius XII gave Wyszyński the extraordinary privilege of having a ready-made list of episcopal candidates whom the pope had approved already with his *placet* ("it is pleasing"). If he were to nominate someone, Wyszyński would send a secret message to Rome with that information, and after receiving the pope's confirmation in code, he would begin the negotiations with the government.

He would initially propose phony names, which the government immediately rejected. Then the primate, after more negotiations, would pretend that he was forced to a second choice and choose the very person he wanted as bishop from the secret list, already approved by the pope. The government, thinking it had won, would accede.

Karol Wojtyla's name never appeared on the secret list of future Polish bishops. Wyszyński respected Wojtyla's training of young people and knew he was appreciated at Lublin University. Perhaps he thought that one day Professor Wojtyla would become chancellor of the university. But he did not consider him suitable to oversee a diocese. However, "someone else" wanted things to go in a different direction, and so they did.

BISHOP WOJTYLA

Bishop Baziak, beaten down by the hardships he endured from the communist party, felt that he did not have much longer to live. He understood Kraków's problems and his adversaries, the communist leaders of the city. He looked around at his aides to see if someone could take his place in such a difficult hour.

Baziak remembered Cardinal Sapieha's esteem for Wojtyla and became convinced that he was the man to keep the Church alive in Kraków and fight the communist regime. He probably spoke to the primate and discovered that Wyszyński was not interested in Wojtyla. Therefore, Baziak decided to insert himself into a matter that was not really his business. He wrote directly to the pope.

What he wrote is not known, but it must have been convincing. At the beginning of July 1958 Wyszyński received a

telegram from Rome signed by Pius XII: "At the request of
Archbishop Baziak, I am appointing Father Karol Wojtyla as
Auxiliary Bishop of Kraków. Kindly send your approval for
this appointment."

Wyszyński read and reread the telegram. This was the first
time someone had gone around him in a decisive way. He
could not understand why this had happened. The pope was
aware of how complicated things had become in Poland
between the Church and state. Why had Pius XII not consulted him rather than sending him a telegram with a specific
directive?

On July 4 Cardinal Wyszyński sent a telegram to Karol
Wojtyla summoning him to Warsaw on an urgent matter.
Professor Wojtyla was vacationing near the Masurian Lakes
with some young people from his group. He received the telegram in the evening when he returned to the campsite after a
day of kayaking and discussion. The next day he told the
young people that he needed to be away for a few days but that
he would return as soon as he could.

He arrived in Warsaw on July 8 and went straight to the
episcopal palace. Wyszyński, after receiving him in his private
office, said he had an interesting letter from the Holy Father.
He read Wojtyla the letter.

Wyszyński wrote in his journal that the general reaction on
the part of candidates to such important assignments was
always the same: shock and then a request to consider the matter for a few days and consult with a spiritual director. These
were understandable attitudes, but they infuriated the cardinal, who was a man of quick action. He would retort in a dry
tone, "If you are a mature person, you should know what you
want to do."[1]

Sometimes candidates would say they needed to pray and
ask Jesus for advice. Wyszyński would reply, "There's a chapel

right behind that door there. Please, say your prayer. But please don't take any more than fifteen minutes, because I don't have the time and neither does Jesus."

Now Wyszyński watched the thirty-eight-year-old priest seated in front of him. Wojtyla was an athletic, tan, healthy young man who seemed very self-confident. The cardinal knew he had interrupted his vacation. "Do you accept the appointment?" he asked.

After a few seconds of silence, Wojtyla said in a mellow and resolute voice, "Where do I sign?"

Half an hour later Karol Wojtyla was knocking at the Ursuline Convent near the cardinal's residence. He asked the nun who answered the door where the chapel was. He went in without a word and knelt in the first pew. One hour, two hours went by, and the priest was still there.

The nuns became curious and went to peek at him. One nun recognized him and said he was a famous professor who taught at Lublin University.

They all gathered around to ask questions. To be teaching in that Catholic university at that time was very prestigious. The nun told them everything she knew. She said he also had a reputation for being a poet and a dramatist.

The Mother Superior waited a little bit and then entered the chapel. Wojtyla was praying with his face in his hands. She invited Karol to join the community for dinner. Wojtyla looked at her. He told her that his train would leave after midnight. He wanted to stay there praying because he had many things to discuss with the Lord.

He left the chapel after 11:30 P.M. to catch his train. Eight hours had gone by since he had knelt down before the tabernacle.

CHAPTER THIRTEEN

A Staunch Bishop

B ISHOP BAZIAK OFFICIATED AT Wojtyla's consecration on September 15, 1958, the feast of St. Wenceslas, in Wawel Cathedral. The new bishop was fairly well known in Kraków for his preaching, teaching, lectures and spiritual retreats for professionals, especially doctors. Crowds of his friends and admirers gathered around him on this festive day to demonstrate their affection.

A very ancient tradition dictates that every new bishop choose a motto for his coat of arms. Generally that saying represents a lifestyle or an ideal of pastoral action. Wojtyla chose *Totus tuus* ("All yours"). These two words are part of the prayer of consecration to Our Lady from St. Louis Maria Grignion de Montfort, the saint he had come to know during his time with Jan Tyranowski in the Living Rosary. Now that Wojtyla was called to exercise the fullness of his priesthood in leading the people of God, he reaffirmed his complete trust in Our Lady.

Not everyone in Kraków, however, was happy with Wojtyla's nomination. Some ultra-conservatives were suspicious of his conduct. The trips to the mountains with young people and engaged couples and his ease in dressing in civilian clothes were criticized. Wojtyla was an "overly modern priest," too open to dialogue with the communists and too social—a priest who could not be trusted.

In actuality his opposition to communism was clear-cut but sensible. He did not proceed with hasty, emotional activity; he met enemies squarely on an intellectual plane with calm composure, always bewildering them. The communists understood that Wojtyla was a difficult opponent, but at the same time they were not able to categorize him correctly. One of the leaders even had the illusion that he could manipulate him, so on certain occasions he showed Wojtyla trust and respect. It was precisely this respectful treatment that alarmed those who had absolutely refused to dialogue with their political adversaries under any circumstances.

IMPORTANT EVENTS

After the festivities Bishop Karol Wojtyla went back to his former life of classes at the university, lectures, retreats, sermons, study, spiritual direction in the confessional and trips to the mountains with his youth groups. He also continued to write poetry and to work on some plays. His days were full. He rose very early and went to bed very late.

Bishop Baziak was accustomed to sacrifices because of his prison experience, so he kept active even as his health was declining. However, his assignments for Wojtyla began to increase. Wojtyla often had to represent Baziak, especially for visits outside Kraków.

On the night of June 14, 1962, Eugeniusz Baziak died at the age of seventy-two. He was buried with great solemnity, and the Polish people chose to place on his tombstone the title that the government had always denied him, "Archbishop of Kraków."

One month later, on July 16, the capitular chapter of the cathedral in Kraków, made up of senior priests, elected Wojtyla "capitular vicar" and temporary administrator of the archdiocese. They wanted the archdiocese of Kraków to function normally until a successor for Baziak was elected. That person would also be the successor to Sapieha, because the Polish government had never ratified Baziak's nomination.

In Rome an extraordinary event was about to begin: the Second Vatican Council. A council is a meeting of all the bishops of the world and the bishop of Rome, the pope, to discuss Church problems. There have only been twenty councils in the Church's history. The previous one, the First Vatican Council, took place in 1870. It was called by Pius IX but suspended because of the occupation of Rome by Italian troops.

Announced by Pope John XXIII on January 25, 1959, the twenty-first Ecumenical Council entailed almost four years of feverish preparation and was attended by all the bishops. The opening was set for October 7, 1962.

This was an opportunity for the bishops in communist countries to go to Rome, though not everyone could go. The Polish delegation consisted of Cardinal Wyszyński and twenty-four bishops. It was Wojtyla's first time outside Poland since 1946, when he was sent to Rome for theology studies.

Wojtyla was happy to be returning to the Eternal City, where he had lived for two years. In Rome he lodged near the Polish College, located on the Aventine Hill in a beautiful, sunny location full of greenery. He enjoyed an overview of the whole city.

Wojtyla was very moved at the Mass for the council's opening in St. Peter's Basilica. In that enormous basilica, the heart

of Christianity, 2,381 council fathers had gathered. Along the
sides of the central nave were ten graduated rows of platforms.
Wojtyla was seated in the section at the entrance of the basilica, since he was a new bishop. From this position he could
observe the entire basilica with its spectacular panorama of
white miters dotted with the round, black headgear of the
patriarchs of the Eastern Church. In a separate section were
101 observers from other Christian denominations and a few
hundred theologians and other scholars.

A FRIEND IN NEED

Bad news arrived in the midst of Wojtyla's joy and contented-
ness. One evening when he returned to the Polish college, he
found a letter from Poland. Dr. Wanda Póltawska, age forty,
the wife of his friend Andrei Póltawsky, was dying.

Wojtyla had known she was ill. When he left Poland her
testing and assessments were still going on, and he thought
that medical science would save her. Instead the cancer in her
tumor had spread throughout her body. The doctors planned
to do surgery, but the hope for recovery was infinitesimal.

Wanda Póltawska never talked about herself, but she was a
person of unequalled spiritual stature. During the war she
had been a real heroine. She underwent horrible torture to
avoid betraying her political friends and unspeakable physical
and moral suffering at Ravensbrück, the infamous Nazi
concentration camp in Germany—all with great faith and res-
ignation. Her short book about the ordeal, *And I Am Afraid of
My Dreams*, is a shocking document.

The horrible experiences that Wanda Póltawska underwent
from age eighteen to twenty-two can literally destroy a person's psychic balance, but not a strong woman whose heart is
secure in her faith. Having survived these horrors, Wanda
decided to dedicate the rest of her life to others. She went back

to school and graduated in medicine with a specialization in psychiatry. She became part of Wojtyla's Circle, married Andrei, a philosophy professor, and had four children.

This lady was one of Wojtyla's closest colleagues. As a doctor and a psychiatrist, she had advised him on marriage and family problems. She had been an invaluable consultant for the draft of his *Love and Responsibility*. Wojtyla had appreciated her faith and Christian commitment.

Now here she was, only forty years old, with four small children, dying. The doctors had given up on her. Wanda wrote that she was hospitalized because of an illness and waiting for surgery which would extend her life for a year or a year and a half as long as the cancer did not metastasize. She agreed to the surgery so as to use every scientific means available, feeling that she needed to live as long as possible since she still had young children.

Wojtyla prayed for his friend and asked his friends to pray. Then he remembered his 1947 visit with Padre Pio of Pietrelcina.

PADRE PIO

At this time Padre Pio was "in disgrace." Two years earlier, in the summer of 1960, Pope John XXIII had authorized an apostolic visit to shed light on some presumably scandalous events involving the monk. They were wretched slanders, as history has proved, but the visit resulted in an unfavorable outcome for the monk. The Holy See issued some very severe disciplinary measures against him—measures that were only used for rebellious priests.

Karol Wojtyla was certainly aware of the situation, but he did not let that deter him. He had his own opinion about Padre Pio, which was unaffected by gossip. He was sure this monk was a man of God, and he trusted in his intervention.

He wrote a short letter in Latin entitled "*Curia metropolitana cracoviensis*" (Diocese of Kraków) and dated November 17, 1962:

> Reverend Father,
>
> I would ask you to pray for a mother of four children who is forty years old and lives in Kraków, Poland. In the last war she was in a concentration camp in Germany for five years, and she is now dying of cancer. Please pray that God, through the intervention of the Most Blessed Virgin, may have mercy on her and her family.
>
> Gratefully yours in Christ,
Karol Wojtyla

The letter reached Angelo Battisti, who was working for the Secretary of State at the Vatican. He had been a "spiritual son" of Padre Pio in the 1940s and had access to the holy monk. He showed me the letters in 1983.

"I think it is time to bring this fact to light," he said. "I am sick and dying, but I want people to know what Padre Pio did for Karol Wojtyla." According to Battisti:

> The letter was given to me by an Italian cardinal, who told me it concerned a matter of utmost importance and I should leave immediately to hand-deliver the letter to Padre Pio. I had never received such an urgent request from the Vatican. I went home, got in my car, and left immediately. When I arrived at San Giovanni Rotondo, I went to Padre Pio's cell. I gave him the letter and said it was urgent.
>
> "Open it and read it to me," he said. He had his head down and, as always, was praying. I opened the envelope and read him the letter. He listened in silence. When I finished reading the few lines, he continued to remain silent. He raised his head and, looking at me with his penetrating eyes, said, "Angiolino, that request cannot be denied."

After eleven days, on November 28, Karol Wojtyla wrote a new letter to Padre Pio:

Reverend Father,

The woman living in Kraków, Poland, the mother of four children, was instantly healed before her surgery on November 21. Thanks be to God! I wish to express profound thanks to you, Reverend Father, on behalf of the lady, her husband and her whole family.

> In Christ,
> Karol Wojtyla
> Capitular Vicar of Kraków

The Vatican asked Angelo Battisti to take this letter also to San Giovanni Rotondo.

I left immediately again this time because the Vatican's tone was still urgent.... I arrived in San Giovanni Rotondo, went into Padre Pio's cell, showed him the letter, and again he said, "Open it and read it to me." This time I read it with great interest too, because I wanted to know what could be so important and, hearing the truly extraordinary and stupendous news, I looked over at Padre Pio to congratulate him. But Padre Pio was immersed in prayer. He seemed not to have heard me as I read the letter. I waited in silence for him to say something or to tell me to return to Rome. After a few minutes, he said, "Angelino, keep those letters because one day they will be important."

I returned to Rome and preserved the letters as Padre Pio told me. Sixteen years had gone by and I almost forgot I had them. But that Monday evening on October 16, 1978, when I heard Cardinal Felici announce to the world from the central balcony of the basilica the name of the new pope elected to replace John Paul I, I was jolted. The new pope was Karol Wojtyla, the Polish bishop who had given me the letter to take to Padre Pio to ask for the healing of the lady in Kraków. I immediately thought of Padre Pio's statement, "That request cannot be denied," and tears came to my eyes.

The unexpected healing of Dr. Póltawska—confirmed by doctors before she went into the operating room—is undoubtedly an astounding thing. Dr. Półtawska is still alive as I write and is quite well.

But what is most pertinent for this book is Padre Pio's statement on hearing Karol Wojtyla's letter read to him, "This request cannot be denied." In November 1962 Karol Wojtyla was a lowly bishop whom no one in Italy knew. What did the holy monk know about him?

Baziak's Successor

At the beginning of 1963, at the first reconvening of the Second Vatican Council, Cardinal Wyszyński began to examine the procedure for naming someone to lead the Kraków diocese. This would be a very sensitive nomination. Cardinal Sapieha had chosen Baziak for this assignment, in agreement with Pius XII, but the communist leader of the city had vetoed it. The Church had not wanted to back down, and so Baziak had acted as head of the diocese, but the episcopal seat of Kraków remained "vacated."

Wyszyński did not want a repeat situation. After Warsaw, Kraków was the most important metropolitan diocese of Poland, and it needed to be fully operational. Wyszyński was looking for a bishop who was equal to this task and whom the government would not veto.

In Kraków everyone expected Bishop Wojtyla to be nominated. The approval expressed by the ecclesiastical authorities there in nominating him as capitular vicar was an obvious act of confidence and an eloquent signal. It was a signal, however, that the primate of the Polish church did not seem to have any intention of following. At that time Wyszyński was indifferent to the philosophy professor who liked to ski and go kayaking with his friends. The primate considered Wojtyla too young, somewhat theoretical, immersed in pedantic philosophical and poetic endeavors and, therefore, hardly suited to oversee a diocese.

This stance on Wyszyński's part would completely change in the following years as he came to know Wojtyla better. During the conclave of 1978 he would be his most authoritative supporter. However, at the beginning of 1963, the two were separated by a wall of misunderstanding and prejudice that seemed insurmountable.

At the beginning of 1963 Primate Wyszyński presented three candidates for the archdiocese of Kraków—Monsignor Wojtyla's name not among them—and the communist government blocked all three. Wyszyński absorbed that blow and prepared another list of names.

Meanwhile, Pope John XXIII died on June 3, 1963. Cardinal Wyszyński went to Rome for the funeral and for the conclave. Archbishop Montini was elected and took the name Paul VI.

During his stay in Rome Wyszyński discussed, among other things, the nomination for the archbishop of Kraków with the Poles who were working at the Vatican. He probably also spoke to the new pope about it. When he returned to his homeland, he had a new list of candidates; Karol Wojtyla's name did not appear on that list either.

In Kraków, on the other hand, people's respect for Wojtyla was growing. Seeing that twice now Wojtyla's name had not been on the roster of candidates, a delegation from the archdiocese went to Warsaw to formally request that the primate consider the capitular vicar.

In October Wyszyński had to return to Rome for the second session of the Second Vatican Council. Before leaving he presented the communist authorities with his third list of candidates. This time Wojtyla's name was included. While he was in Rome, Wyszyński learned that the communists had selected Wojtyla.

A COMMUNIST PLOT

The communist leaders had a specific political goal in selecting Wojtyla. They were aware that there was little rapport between the primate in Warsaw and the professor at Lublin. They thought that Wojtyla would oppose the primate and thus play into their hands. Furthermore, they thought that Wojtyla was malleable and conciliatory. He was a young man, a poet, someone not given to politics—a person, in their opinion, who could be used against the primate, whom they considered an intractable, rigid man.

The man who did more than anyone else to bring down communism was moved along in his ecclesiastical career by the communists themselves. It is said that the leader of the communist party in Kraków, Zenon Kliszko, boasted that he had personally blocked the six candidates Wyszyński presented on the first two lists. He also declared in public several times that he had almost sent a message to Primate Wyszyński: "Oh, give us Wojtyla, or you will never get the 'placet' from us for anyone else."

The warden of the prison in Dantzig had a famous detainee among his prisoners, the Benedictine abbot Piotr Rosworowski. When the communist warden learned about Wojtyla's election, he went to the abbot's cell and gloated, "Finally, some good news." Only four months later he returned to the cell to tell the abbot, "That Wojtyla betrayed us!"

A document from the secret service of the communist regime in those years states:

> It can safely be said that he [Wojtyla] is one of the few intellectuals in the Polish Episcopate.... He has not, so far, engaged in open anti-state political activity.... He lacks organizing and leadership qualities, and this is his weakness in the rivalry with Wyszyński.... We must encourage Wojtyla's interest in the overall problems of the Polish Church, and assist him in handling problems with his archdiocese.... And we must continue to demonstrate our ill-will

toward Wyszyński at every opportunity, but not in a way that would force Wojtyla to show solidarity with Wyszyński.[1]

The communists made an error in their calculations because they understood nothing about Karol Wojtyla. Father Andrzej Bardecki, the religion editor of *Tygodnik*, wrote, "The Holy Spirit can bring his will to pass by 'darkening' as well as by enlightening men's minds."

CHAPTER FOURTEEN

New Power in Kraków

P OPE PAUL VI CONFIRMED Karol Wojtyla's nomination as
archbishop of Kraków on December 30, 1963. The announcement was made public on January 19, with the solemn instal-
lation following on March 8.

Wojtyla planned a ceremony full of significant historical
and religious symbolism. He wore the golden chasuble given
to the archdiocese by Anna Jagiellon, the wife of King Stefan
Batory. On top of that he wore a pallium donated by Queen
Jadwiga in the sixteenth century. The mitre had belonged to
Andrzej Lipski, a seventeenth-century bishop. The crozier
dated back to the reign of Jan Sobieski, the king who defeated
the Turks in the Battle of Vienna in 1683. His ring belonged to
the fourth successor of St. Stanislaw, Bishop Mauritius, who
died in 1118. The chalice for the Mass was the one used during the time of the Jagiellonian dynasty.

Before entering the cathedral Wojtyla reverently kissed the
relics of St. Stanislaw that were brought to him. Entering the
Gothic cathedral, he stopped to pray at the sepulcher of

St. Stanislaw and at the Black Cross of the Blessed Queen Jadwiga. Finally he prayed at the chapel of the Blessed Sacrament. He kissed the altar and then sat on the throne, the episcopal "cathedra," where he received the homage of auxiliary bishops, priests and other religious authorities. Then he addressed the crowded cathedral.

He spoke about his feeling, in that very time and place, where "the whole history, the whole of our nation's past" was so vitally present. He explained the task he had received from the pope. He planned to fulfill that task but not, as leaders of nations sometimes do, with five-year plans. His plan was "the eternal programme of God and Jesus Christ." He intended to fulfill that plan "with increased zeal and increased readiness," following the procedure for renewal outlined by the Second Vatican Council.[1]

Karol Wojtyla was not yet forty-four years old. He understood the importance of the grave responsibility entrusted to him by the Church, and he was committed wholeheartedly to fulfilling his duty.

CREATIVE CONFRONTATIONS

The first to realize this were the leaders of the communist party. Shortly after the solemn ceremony on March 8, 1964, Wojtyla decided to send a pastoral letter to the diocese on the occasion of Lent. Several hundred copies were needed for the parishes and for the religious communities. The government did not give him permission to print the letter.

Wojtyla did not lose time trying to negotiate. He mobilized a group of nuns to type the letter. In a couple of days, working day and night, they prepared hundreds of copies. Wojtyla then had the letter hand-delivered to each church, knowing the post office had been ordered to sabotage any correspondence from Catholic organizations.

Wojtyla had a rare capacity to understand the communists' rules and to challenge them. He was unperturbed by any influence that was contrary to his vocation. Despite grave danger and fearful threats, Wojtyla would go his own way, and no one could stop him.

The communists' expectations in encouraging his candidacy collapsed. Zenon Kliszko, the head of the Polish party, left a face-to-face encounter frustrated and confused.

Cardinal Wyszyński also realized, pleasantly, that Wojtyla was very different than he had thought. The intelligent and charismatic primate would soon recognize Wojtyla as his heir apparent.

In October 1964 the Polish bishops returned to Rome for another session of the Second Vatican Council, and the new archbishop stood out in this setting as well. Karol Wojtyla gave seven speeches in plenary sessions and presented thirteen written declarations. During the complicated and difficult discussions on issues that divided the assembly, Wojtyla exercised a decisive role as mediator, demonstrating maturity and an extraordinary capacity for dialogue and persuasion.

Pope Paul VI was very appreciative of the archbishop's interventions. When the council ended he wanted to get to know him better. Wyszyński remained the official primate, but Wojtyla became the pope's reference point for the problems of the Polish Church. Wojtyla also would give Paul VI valuable support in the definitive draft of the encyclical *Humanae Vitae*. In one meeting the pope demonstrated his esteem by giving Wojtyla a stone taken from St. Peter's tomb.

Millennium Celebration

In 1966 Poland was to celebrate a thousand years of Christian history. The Polish Church wanted to give preeminence to this anniversary by calling the faithful to reflection on their religious roots. Wojtyla's power in resisting the communist regime came into play.

It was an unusual kind of power. He was not an emotionally charged, political anti-communist. His opposition was on the rational and philosophical level. His concept of human beings and their dignity was exactly the opposite of that of Marxist-Leninist ideology. The communists were children of God and therefore his brothers and sisters—brothers and sisters, however, who were full of error and bent on a destructive mission that had to be absolutely rejected.

The communists were trying to eradicate religious and civil traditions. They wanted a people without roots, without strength and without a unique character. The archbishop decided to make an appeal to history, traditions and the glorious past. He knew that by doing so the Polish people would become united, including the new generations that had embraced communist ideology.

He sought to maintain the celebration of patron saint feast days, traditional pilgrimages to shrines and processions. The regime had tried to abolish the procession for Corpus Christi, commemorating the Eucharist. The Church, overwhelmingly supported by the people, opposed its abolition but was forced to yield somewhat. The procession was limited to the streets in the church's neighborhood.

Archbishop Wojtyla decided that the nexus of the celebration of the thousand years of Christianity would be the most famous Polish Marian shrine at Czestochowa, where the "Black Madonna" is venerated as the Queen of Poland. The Black Madonna is a very ancient painting on wood. According to tradition, Luke the evangelist, a doctor and artist, painted this depiction of Our Lady when she was still alive. After numerous mishaps in the East, in 326 the painting fell into the hands of St. Helena during her pilgrimage to Jerusalem. The queen gave it to her son, the Emperor Constantine, who brought it to Constantinople. There it became famous for numerous miracles that were attributed to it.

During the period of iconoclasm, the painting was hidden to avoid its destruction. Around 980 the painting went to Kiev, in the Ukraine. Anna, the sister of the Emperor Basil II, included this painting as part of her dowry when she married Vladimir, the prince of Kiev. In 988 Prince Vladimir and his people converted to Christianity, and the painting became part of the treasury of Russian princes. They in turn gave it to the Orthodox Church. In 1382 Ladislaw, the prince of Poland and viceroy of Leopoli, removed the painting from a Basilian monastery and placed it at the monastery in Czestochowa, where it is today.

The painting is a symbol of the history of Poland. Throughout the centuries Poles have prayed before it when they were in difficulty, and Our Lady, "Queen of Poland," has always protected them. Every Polish person has made a pilgrimage to Czestochowa at least once.

Wojtyla had a copy of the painting made and sent it on procession throughout the whole country—to cities, parishes and families. Wherever it went people welcomed the image devotedly. They sensed the meaning of that symbolic pilgrimage by the Mother to her children.

The communist leaders needed to retaliate for this humiliation. They organized counterdemonstrations in the cities as the Black Madonna arrived, but these did not capture the people's attention. Then they prohibited processions of sacred images. The copy of the Black Madonna was returned to Czestochowa.

Wojtyla then ordered that the processions continue but with only the empty frame. That move was like a bombshell. Huge crowds gathered to welcome the empty frame, and people wept because the Queen of Poland could not visit her people. Wojtyla took part in fifty-seven of these displays and gave impassioned speeches on history, the right to religious freedom and human dignity.

The culmination for the celebration was set for May 3 at the shrine of Czestochowa. Pope Paul VI was to be present, but the government refused him a visa. Again Wojtyla found a way to turn the situation into a celebration of faith for the believers and a blow to his political opponents. He had an empty papal throne placed next to the altar, and all the participants received a leaflet with the message:

> We see the pontifical throne next to the altar. Pope Paul VI was supposed to be with us today. He wanted to celebrate the Eucharist and address us in Polish. Even though all of us invited him by telegrams and letters, he was not able to come because Jesus, who dwells in the church in the person of the pope, was not invited by the authorities in our country. He was barred from coming to Poland and from receiving our famous hospitality.

BUILDING CHURCHES

The Church was prohibited from establishing new parishes and building new churches without the government's permission. Every year Wojtyla presented an average of thirty requests for building permits for churches or parish buildings, which the government would deny categorically. The following year Wojtyla would present the same thirty requests, rephrasing them. Wojtyla kept the people informed, and the repeated refusals by the leaders made them look like harsh dictators.

As the government built new districts and new cities without churches, Wojtyla invited courageous priests to do door-to-door ministry and to gather the faithful outdoors on Sunday—in fields or in big courtyards—to celebrate Mass. He personally celebrated Mass on important religious feast days in communities that had no churches. After a while, when these meetings had become habitual, he would tell the government that in a given area there was a "*de facto* parish." He would ask that it be recognized and allowed a church building.

The government would ignore or reject the request, but Wojtyla would continue the attack with methodical persistence. He was always on the people's side—defending the rights of the workers, the unemployed, the poor, the Jews, the intellectuals and the marginalized of every kind—so the government was the loser from the start.

Wojtyla's persistent, nagging strategy paid off. From 1962 to 1978, before he was elected pope, he succeeded in setting up eleven new parishes and ten new "parish centers," which were waiting to become parishes.

One of the longest and hardest fought battles concerned Nowa Huta, the model city for workers built on the outskirts of Kraków. The new city was full of enormous apartment buildings, some of which had 450 apartments. Each building was comprised of units that did not connect to each other, and every unit had three or four apartments. If someone wanted to visit a neighbor who lived just a few yards away in the adjacent unit, he or she had to descend to the street level, enter the unit where the neighbor lived, then take the stairs or the elevator up to the friend's place. It was like making a trip, practically speaking, and that discouraged people from communicating with their neighbors. Five thousand people lived in Nowa Huta in 1951; twenty years later there were 170,000 people.

Wojtyla proceeded to create a "*de facto* parish." Every year he would celebrate Christmas Mass there in the field near the immense concrete beehive. Every year the crowd attending this Mass under the stars increased.

On October 13, 1967, four months after he became a cardinal, he succeeded in obtaining authorization to build a church. The government could no longer deny the requests that Wojtyla had been sending for years. The cardinal presided at the opening ceremony at the site and swung the first pick-axe to dig the foundation.

The design for the new church had been ready for some time. Wojtyla had wanted a structure in the shape of an ark, which would symbolize Our Lady, "Queen of Poland," as the Ark of the Covenant who saves her people. The church was even called the "Church of the Ark." He incorporated into the foundation the stone from St. Peter's tomb at the Vatican that Paul VI had given him.

The church is a masterpiece of solidarity. Construction took ten years of volunteer labor from all over Poland and other European countries. It was hindered in a thousand ways by the governing authorities but never halted.

The outside is decorated with two million polished pebbles from Polish riverbeds. The inside is dominated by a large steel crucifix forged by workers at the Lenin steel mill in Nowa Huta. The tabernacle, donated by the diocese of St. Pòlten in Austria, is in the shape of the solar system, and its decoration includes a fragment of a lunar rock given to Pope Paul VI by an American astronaut. The bells are a gift from the Dutch people.

At its consecration on May 15, 1977, the cardinal gave a very harsh speech against the government in defense of humanity and the individual. He said of Nowa Huta: "This is not a city...of people to whom one may do whatever one wants, who may be manipulated according to the laws or rules of production and consumption. This is a city of the children of God."[2]

The fight over the construction of Nowa Huta's church is one of many battles won by Karol Wojtyla in Poland during the communist regime. He became a thorn in the government's side. He was a philosopher with arguments on end to counter all the sophist arguments of the politicians; he was a poet with endless creative ideas for traps and snares against the bureaucracy; he was an actor who could present the dramatic suffering and humiliation of his people; and he gave speeches that stirred souls. The communist regime treated him with uneasy respect.

CHAPTER FIFTEEN

A Pope from a Distant Country

ACCORDING TO HIS AIDES, Cardinal Wojtyla's daily life in Kraków followed a strenuous schedule. At 5:30 A.M. he was in his private chapel. At 7:00 he went to the Franciscan church across the street and prayed. At 8:00 he returned for breakfast. Then he would go to his chapel, close the door and work until 11:00. On the left side of the chapel he had built for himself a wooden chair with a kneeler and a desk so that he could write and pray at the same time. After 11:00 he would receive whoever wanted to speak with him. Lunch was at 1:30, and afternoons were dedicated to visiting the 329 parishes in the archdiocese. Evenings were for discussions with his friends and aides about the problems of the Polish Church.

He became a very popular personality in Poland. Though the iron curtain blocked knowledge of him outside of Poland, his activity on behalf of the Polish Church and his literary works were known in certain intellectual circles in the West. He was especially known for *Person and Act*, his most important philosophical work, which is now part of the body of twentieth-century philosophical thought.

Cardinal Wojtyla was invited to give lectures in the United States, Australia and various European countries. He frequently went to Italy to stay at the Vatican, where for some years he delivered the spiritual exercises for the pope and the pontifical curia.

A NEW FRIEND

During these trips he would occasionally visit Venice and its patriarch, Albino Luciani, with whom he had become friends. They also corresponded by mail. A friend of the Luciani family collected foreign stamps, so the Venice patriarch would always send her the envelopes he received from foreign countries. After Wojtyla's election to the papacy, the woman realized she had seven envelopes from the hand of Wojtyla.

In the spring of 1977 Cardinal Albino Luciani, patriarch of Venice, led a pilgrimage to Fatima. Rumor has it that Sister Lucia, the last survivor of the three seers at Fatima, told him at that time that he would reign briefly as pope and be succeeded by the cardinal of Kraków. The story is still circulating and perhaps has some foundation.

On August 6, 1978, Paul VI died at Castel Gandolfo. The funeral was held on August 13, and on August 28 the cardinals began their conclave. It lasted only one day, one of the shortest conclaves in history. Albino Luciani was elected.

The Catholic world was faced with an unexpected, physically fragile, simple pope with an honest and endearing smile. But after thirty-two days tragedy struck. On the morning of September 29, Sister Vincenza, who usually brought the pope his coffee, went into his bedroom and found him dead. The doctors said he died of a heart attack, but mysterious rumors still swirl around the event.

Cardinal Jaime Sin, the archbishop of Manila, stated publicly in his home city the day before that Pope John Paul I had told him, "My pontificate will be short." A few days before his death he had confided to Sister Vincenza, who was his nurse for years, that he would not remain on the throne long because a foreigner soon would sit upon it. At supper two nights before this he told his secretary, Monsignor John Magee:

> There were others better than I, and Paul VI had already indicated his successor. During the conclave that successor was across the hall from me at the Sistine Chapel. But he will soon understand why I need to go away.[1]

The room across from Luciani's during the conclave was occupied by Karol Wojtyla.

It is said that Wojtyla received the news of Pope John Paul's death when he was about to have coffee. He became pale and dropped his spoon. He did not say a word but withdrew to his private chapel, where he stayed for quite a long time. In the subsequent hours he wrote what seems to be his last poem, "Stanislaw." Afterward he explained that he wrote it "to pay my debt to Kraków." The poem's theme is martyrdom and is a farewell to Kraków. It is said that while he was writing it, the pen broke in his hand.

ELECTION

On October 2, 1978, Wojtyla left Kraków for Warsaw. The next day he flew to Rome with Cardinal Wyszyński. They arrived at the Vatican around 1:00 P.M. and went to St. Peter's Basilica to pay homage to the body of John Paul I. On October 14 at 4:30 P.M., after the Mass of the Holy Spirit at St. Peter's, the 111 cardinals who were to elect the next pope began the conclave. Wojtyla was almost late because he went to visit a friend.

It is uncertain what really happened during the conclave because the cardinals are bound to secrecy. However, a few facts leaked out. There were two candidates who seemed to be the favorites: Cardinal Giovanni Benelli, the archbishop of Florence, who was already a deputy to the Secretary of State at the Vatican, and Cardinal Giuseppe Siri, the archbishop of Genoa.

In the first vote it seems that Benelli received 75 of the 111 votes. He was within an inch of the election but could not cross the threshold of required votes. The cardinals considered the possibility of a pope who did not come from Italy. Karol Wojtyla had received a handful of votes during the previous conclave; his name was once again proposed.

On the morning of October 16 Wojtyla received a significant number of votes. At lunch he appeared tense and preoccupied. After lunch he was seen in an agitated state in Cardinal Wyszyński's room. It seems that Cardinal Wyszyński had told him not to refuse if they elected him. Wojtyla fell into the primate's arms and burst into tears.

During the seventh vote he was elected, but he refused. On the eighth vote he received 104 out of 111 votes. He could not withdraw from his duty. Yet a few hours after being presented to the people, he admitted, he was afraid to accept the office.

The last non-Italian pope was Adrian IV, a Dutchman, whose election was in 1522. Immediately after the conclave, Cardinal John Krol is reported to have said to the media that if they hadn't foreseen this outcome, they weren't the only ones.

A POPULAR POPE

Pope John Paul II quickly became popular throughout the world. Newspapers and television helped, but it was also his personality and sports-loving, nonconformist lifestyle that made him loved. He looked like an athlete. His voice, delivery and gestures were those of an actor; his ideas, plans and projects were those of an innovative, highly cultured intellectual. He spoke eight languages and had a creative imagination.

But it was especially his physical presence that charmed people. The day after the conclave he left the confines of the Vatican to visit a sick friend at Gemelli General Hospital. One week later he flew by helicopter to the monastery at Mentorella, about thirty miles from Rome, where he had prayed when he was a cardinal. When he met the mayor of Rome, a member of the communist party, he embraced him. He received Archbishop Lefebvre, who was suspended *a divinis* ("from all priestly and episcopal powers").

He decided to make a trip to Mexico, an anticlerical country where priests were prohibited from wearing cassocks and there were no diplomatic relations with the Holy See. His aides, including the Secretary of State, learned about that decision from the newspapers. He went to Santo Domingo and Mexico at the end of January 1979.

In June he traveled to Poland; in September to Ireland; in October to the United States; and at the end of November to Turkey. Pope Paul VI had made nine trips outside of Italy in fifteen years; Pope John Paul II made five in one year, gathering such immense crowds that one American newspaper wrote, "He is the most visible personality of the year."

The pope's every word, thanks to his popularity, reached wide audiences. But not everyone liked him.

The Troublesome Revolutionary

In December 1979 I came to Rome to do a comprehensive article on the pope's first year. The article was supposed to reflect the wonder, the surprise, the novelty and the success of John Paul II. I met with a variety of sources in Rome, and a troubling picture emerged. Although the pope thrilled the people, it became clear that certain powerful groups were not happy.

"John Paul II's success, his influence on crowds and especially on young people is, for some people, disturbing, annoying and worrisome," said a Polish monsignor, a friend of the pope who did not want his name published.

I approached a well-known journalist and author, Benny Lai. He was an expert in the politics of the Holy See and of the Vatican, with more than thirty years of experience in the traditions of the papal palaces. He also enjoyed the trust of quite a few cardinals. According to Lai,

> There are hard times ahead for Pope Wojtyla. The crowds love him, but some powerful groups oppose him. Criticism is spreading and on the increase. It is my impression that these critics, coming from the right and the left, are about to join forces, and so difficult days are coming. Pope Wojtyla has had his Palm Sunday, his day of triumph, but Passion Week is now approaching.
>
> He is a troublesome pope for everybody. The conservatives and the liberals don't like him, the Curia doesn't like him, and he is regarded with suspicion by Catholic agencies. Logically, he was not the ideal person for the cardinals at the conclave to pick. Insofar as I can tell, the cardinals wanted an elderly, moderate, Italian pope; this one is young, active and foreign.

Benny Lai's comments had some foundation. From the time Wojtyla arrived, change was on the agenda. It seemed that an invigorating wind was blowing through every department, congregation, prefecture and office of the Vatican. Things were going full steam in a way no one had seen before. Overtime became necessary. Everything happening around Pope John Paul II was spontaneous and seemingly without limits.

The most serious accusation against the Polish pope was that in one year of his papacy, nothing concrete had been accomplished. During his first twelve months the pope was absent from Rome for one and a half months. Additional time was spent in preparing for his trips and for the speeches he personally wrote in Polish and then translated into various languages. On a practical level, he had no time to govern. Because the Church is monolithic and the pope needs to make all the decisions, business was at a standstill.

Critics said that on his trips John Paul II had the attendance of millions of people but not their loyalty. He went to Ireland, but the terrorism continued; he went to America, but the problems troubling the Catholic community there continued; he went to the United Nations, but his appeals did not achieve any result.

They called him "the 'no' pope" during the first year of his papacy. He said "no" to abortion, divorce, the pill, women's ordination, homosexuality, marriage for priests and premarital sex. Thus he drew the anger of all the movements committed to demanding various rights and freedoms.

In America the discussion became heated over the book *The Church and Homosexuality* by the Jesuit John J. McNeill. The author maintained that the Church should approach homosexual and heterosexual relations in the same way.

In Rome the Schillebeeckx case was under review. The Congregation for the Doctrine of the Faith had asked the Dutch theologian for clarification on some of his theological positions. Avant-garde movements sharply accused the pope of wanting a return to a "rigid and absurd" conservatism.

Breaking the Rules

The conservatives were not on John Paul II's side either. They were shocked because he had broken certain stereotypical

patterns and rules considered sacred. They criticized his personal behavior and his style of working without the bureaucracy, as he would often personally intervene to settle
problems without recourse to traditional channels. He had
received the rebellious Archbishop Lefebvre without infor-
mating anyone in the Vatican, not even the Secretary of State.

Critics found his work schedule outrageous. Prior popes
had held audiences in the morning, but John Paul II held them
in the afternoon and even during the evening.

It had been the custom for the pope to have lunch in his
apartment with his secretary, but John Paul II always had
guests, sometimes five or six. He would invite guests at the last
minute, causing a burden for the nuns who were in charge of
serving. Because the kitchen in the papal apartment was not
equipped for so many guests, John Paul II would go to the
Ospizio di Santa Anna (St. Anne's Hospice) inside the Vatican,
where traveling priests and monsignors were accommodated.
During his vacation the pope had about thirty permanent
guests in his summer residence at Castle Gandolfo, shocking
the entire Curia.

John Paul II was also criticized for keeping up with everything the media said about him. If there were television shows
about him, he wanted to see them. He would often write the
people involved to clarify or correct what was said. He wanted
ongoing relationships with them and gathered enormous
amounts of information on a variety of issues. He was, in a
word, a workhorse who wore out his aides, and many of them
chafed at the bit.

Then came the question of the swimming pool. The pope
initially asked for two pools to be built, one at the Vatican and
one at Castel Gandolfo. When told that perhaps it was not
appropriate for a pope to spend money for sports activities
while so many people in the world were dying from hunger,

John Paul II answered, "What costs more? A pool or another conclave?" He made it clear that he wanted a pool for his health and one was built at Castel Gandolfo.

The news about the pope's pool was made public by anonymous letters from some subordinates who were dissatisfied with their low salaries. It is true that salaries for people working at the Vatican were frozen in 1969, except for annual adjustments for the cost of living, and they were somewhat low. But one has to take into account that none of these employees paid taxes, and they received quite a few benefits.

Some newspapers played up the issue. Pope John Paul II was very sensitive to the problem. He allowed, for the first time in the Vatican, the establishment of a Workers' Committee, the equivalent of a labor union.

DIFFICULT BATTLES

I realized that the environment in which John Paul II worked was not positive toward him. "Even those of us who are journalists," said Benny Lai, "were happy at first because this pope was giving us an enormous amount of material for our articles. But then we began to be too demanding." According to Lai:

> On a return trip from Turkey on the pope's airplane, an unpleasant incident occurred. John Paul II used to spend part of the trip with the journalists, stopping to talk to everyone. It was a highly democratic gesture on his part and very helpful for us. On this trip he had left his compartment, had gone through the cardinals' compartment, and was facing about sixty reporters, photographers, and radio and video personnel.
>
> As soon as he appeared, the people in the first row stood up and began bombarding him with questions and preventing him from answering. The journalists who were left out began to complain. One German reporter shouted out, "This isn't fair!" The pope replied, "The behavior of these reporters is not fair, but neither is it fair to protest in that manner." He turned around and left for his compartment.

His gesture provoked an unthinkable reaction. Terrible swearing and the most indecent expressions were hurled in the pope's direction in many different languages. He probably did not hear them because he was too far away, but the cardinals in the adjoining compartment had to put up with the blasphemous display all the way to Rome.

Paul VI had taken power away from the College of Cardinals. John Paul II had instead given them back their traditional importance, even to those who were over eighty. A month later, the pope called a core group of cardinals to Rome to discuss the finances of the Vatican State for the first time, an issue never broached by any prior pope. The cardinals wanted to know everything about the financial administration of the church, and the pope authorized those in charge to furnish all the explanatory documentation. This was an extremely important action that would have significant consequences later.

Another action that was extremely important to me had to do with the pope's last trip to Turkey. His detractors proclaimed with satisfaction that it was a failed visit because the public did not participate. No crowd, no speeches, no enthusiasm. However, that trip initiated a genuine dialogue for unity with the Orthodox and was the first move in fulfilling a plan that the pope had outlined during his trip to Poland, i.e., the reuniting of Eastern and Western Europe under the banner of Christianity. I am sure one of the destinations for Pope Wojtyla's trips will be Moscow, even if that visit is not imminent.

It is clear as day that this kind of *Ostpolitik* on Pope Wojtyla's part will not be harmful to people who are persecuted for their faith. No one can accuse him on that point since John Paul II lived his life under the communist regime. However, there are vital interests in play, and there are forces that are trying to do everything they can to block the completion of his plan.

The news circulated in Rome that Polish and Russian authorities were planning to thwart the pope's popularity in communist countries through counterfeit news. It was said that an international information agency had been established, headquartered in Rome, whose purpose was to gather and disseminate whatever could in any way discredit the pontiff. A Polish reporter who was part of this agency, confiding to an Italian colleague, said:

> My assignment is tough. When I sit down at my desk to write, I don't know what to write. My articles are supposed to follow three guidelines: I can't speak well of the pope because my government has forbidden that; I can't speak evil of him because civil war would break out in Poland; and I can't remain silent because he is the most famous Pole in the world.

During my investigations I also approached the theologian and writer Claudio Sorgi, today a monsignor teaching at the Lateran Pontifical University but at that time a young journalist on Wojtyla's side. In his opinion:

> The major reactions against the pope had to do with his positions on the basic truths of Christianity. Through a decree from the Congregation for the Doctrine of the Faith, the pope called the world's attention to the soul's existence after death, the resurrection of the dead (which for the church refers to the whole person), and the truths of faith about heaven, purgatory, and hell. In many cultural circles, even Catholic ones, these ideas are considered old-fashioned—stuff from the Middle Ages—but they are really fundamentally important for genuine spirituality. These concepts affirm that the metaphysical reality of a human being is not based on his earthly life, but on his heavenly one. Therefore, all the ideologies tied to materialism must be condemned, but it's clear that doing so causes much consternation. This is the field on which difficult battles will be fought in the coming years. It is the battlefield where good and evil meet—or God and the Evil One— just as the pope himself emphasized on the feast of the Immaculate Heart in the church of St. Mary Major, affirming that "Hard times, times of conflict, are at the gates."

"HE LOVES"

"You always travel with the pope," I said to Benny Lai, "so you can observe him up close. What, in your opinion, is the secret of his appeal to people?" He answered:

I believe the secret of his appeal is his goodness. He is a man who is not afraid of his emotions. He loves, and people can sense that. He suffers, and people can sense that too. The crowd understands that these are honest emotions and continues to be attracted to him. Every person, even in the middle of a multitude of people, has the sense of being loved by him individually. It's a psychological phenomenon that is difficult to explain, but anyone who has followed the pope has experienced it.

I was present for many occasions to witness the extraordinary goodness of the pope in meetings with people. One incident that I will never forget occurred during his visit to the Church of the Holy Cross in Jerusalem here in Rome. As he walked around inside greeting various parish groups, he stopped in front of an elderly lady who was holding the hand of her adult handicapped son. She began to tell her story calmly but still with excruciating pain.

She had been a widow for many years and was ill. Afraid to die since she was the sole support for her son, she asked the pope to pray that her son would die at least a few hours before she did. The pope stood still as he listened to the tragic story. Little by little as the woman spoke, his face became sad. He did not say a word. With tears streaming down his face he caressed the faces of the mother and her son and then blessed them.

Another incident that made an impact on me happened during a visit to the Ospedale del Bambino Gesù [Infant Jesus Hospital] on Christmas last year. The pope stopped at every bed. There was a baby girl whose face was completely disfigured by a tumor, and knowing she only had a few days to live, he took her in his arms and stayed with her a long time, cuddling her just as a father would.

Particularly when he is with sick people, the pope displays an enormous generosity of heart. Tenderness overcomes him, and often his face is bathed in tears.

CHAPTER SIXTEEN

One Hand Shoots, Another Hand Saves

O<small>N</small> M<small>AY</small> 13, 1981, at 5:00 P.M. John Paul II went to St. Peter's Square for his Wednesday general audience. Standing in his white jeep crossing through the square of forty thousand faithful from around the world, he stopped to shake hands and bless babies. At 5:17 he was handing a little girl back to her father when two shots were heard. The pontiff collapsed into the arms of his secretary, Monsignor Stanlislaw Dziewisz, groaning in pain. His white cassock was bloody from the waist up.

Pictures of the Holy Father falling backward from the force of the hit were transmitted on television throughout the world. The incident remains one of the most dramatic historical events of the twentieth century, but it is also one of the most enigmatic and mysterious in many regards. John Paul II said later, "One hand fired the shot…and another one guided the bullet."[1] In other words, an invisible presence intervened to prevent the bullet from hitting his vital organs.

Alì Agca, a twenty-three-year-old Turk, had shot from a distance of less than twenty feet. One bullet had entered the pope's right elbow, and the other had passed through his left index finger and lodged in his stomach.

The jeep driver took off like a rocket. The nearest ambulance was parked next to the Bronze Door, but it was not equipped as a resuscitation unit. The pope was brought to a second ambulance. He was at Policlinico Gemelli (Gemelli General Hospital) in fifteen minutes.

He was bleeding profusely. His blood pressure plunged, and his pulse was barely perceptible. His secretary administered Extreme Unction to an unconscious Holy Father. He was immediately taken to the operating room. When Dr. Francesco Crucitti, the head surgeon at Gemelli, made the first incision, he found "blood, a lot of blood, maybe six pints."

The pope had lost 60 percent of his blood. The doctors needed to aspirate the blood in order to find the source of the hemorrhaging, which was the most imminent danger. Then he was given transfusions to stabilize him enough to allow surgery.

Examining the pope's abdomen, Dr. Crucitti found several lesions, some caused by the explosion of the bullet and some by its path into the stomach. The bullet had perforated the colon and caused five wounds in the small intestine.

Karol Wojtyla was in surgery for five hours. Twenty-two inches of his colon were removed. At 12:45 A.M. on May 14 the doctors issued a bulletin saying the surgery had been successful and the patient's condition was satisfactory.

MARY'S TRIUMPH

John Paul II spent four days in the recovery room. When he was out of danger, he asked Dr. Crucitti for details about the surgery. The doctor confirmed the fact that he had been quite alarmed at the pope's condition. He added that he observed something absolutely unusual and inexplicable.

The bullet had zigzagged on its way to the pope's stomach, missing the vital organs. If it had hit the aorta, which it missed by a hair, the Holy Father would have bled to death before reaching the hospital. If the bullet had hit the nervous system, John Paul II would have been paralyzed. The doctor concluded it seemed as if the bullet had been guided so as to avoid irreparable damage. His words caught the pope's attention.

Someone had noted that the assassination attempt occurred on May 13, the anniversary of the first appearance of the Blessed Mother at Fatima. This coincidence made a strong impression on the pope. He recalled that the file on the third part of the secret of Fatima, which had not been revealed, was still at the Vatican. He had the file brought to him and read it in the hospital.

He was especially struck by the central part. Sister Lucia, referring to the vision that she, Francisco and Jacinta had received on July 13, 1917, had written that they saw a "Bishop dressed in white":

> We had the impression that it was the Holy Father. Other Bishops, Priests, men and women Religious [were] going up a steep mountain, at the top of which there was a big Cross of rough-hewn trunks as of a cork-tree with the bark; before reaching there the Holy Father passed through a big city half in ruins and half trembling with halting step, afflicted with pain and sorrow, he prayed for the souls of the corpses he met on his way; having reached the top of the mountain, on his knees at the foot of the big Cross he was killed by a group of soldiers who fired bullets and arrows at him.[2]

Karol Wojtyla meditated on these words for a long time. He read and reread the first two parts of the secret, about the end of World War I, the beginning of World War II and the birth of atheistic materialism in Russia, a country that would "spread her errors throughout the world, causing wars and persecutions of the Church. The good will be martyred; the Holy Father will have much to suffer; various nations will be annihilated. In the end, my Immaculate Heart will triumph." John Paul II contacted Sister Lucia for further clarifications.

He recognized himself as the "Bishop dressed in white." He realized that certain events in his life had been foreseen even before his birth. He recognized the historical events Our Lady described in 1917 to the visionaries, especially those linked to "atheistic materialism," as he had lived in a communist country. John Paul II was certain that his life had been saved by the extraordinary intervention of Our Lady of Fatima.

THE WORK OF THE ENEMY

Meanwhile, people around the assassin had tried to grab him, but it was a nun who succeeded. The assassin later said that she had enormous strength, with hands like pincers. She managed to pin him down by herself. It was later discovered that the nun bore the same name as one of the visionaries of Fatima, Sister Lucia.

Italian magistrates and secret services from around the world began to investigate the young Turk. They were interested especially in who had hired him. The Turks? The Bulgarians? The Soviets? The Americans? Even in the Vatican there were investigations of what had happened.

The pope was not interested in these questions. Four days after the attack, on a Sunday, he said through a loudspeaker to the crowd waiting outside the hospital, "Pray for the brother who shot me; I have sincerely forgiven him."[3]

As time went on, he still did not want to know how the investigation was going nor to follow the trial of Alì Agca. When his friend Cardinal Deskur asked him why he was completely uninterested in those details, he answered firmly, "It doesn't interest me; because it was the devil who did this thing. And the devil can conspire in a thousand ways, none of which interest me."[4]

Now that the pope recognized himself as the "Bishop dressed in white," he could look on the various dangers he had escaped throughout his life and the tortuous path his vocation had followed and see that a maternal hand had guided, protected and led him. Indeed, when it was necessary, that hand had intervened miraculously to stop the work of the enemy.

The pope understood and accepted the mission that had been entrusted to him. That acceptance had always been implied in his desire to respond to God's call, but now the story's plot was being disclosed. He saw before him the "steep mountain" and wondered if this referred to being shot or if there would be other times ahead. Nevertheless, it was his responsibility to reach that mountain. The secret points to the mystery of salvific suffering, redemptive suffering, Calvary and the mystery of Christ.

A New Danger

John Paul II was in the hospital for twenty days. He returned to the Vatican on June 3. Almost immediately a new danger arose: He had a serious infection in his right lung.

On June 10 his temperature was almost 104 degrees. He was given antibiotics and other special medications, but they were ineffective. He became increasingly weak; his face was sallow, and his eyes were sunken. On July 12 there was a frantic medical consultation at the Vatican. The doctors tried a new treatment, but again there was no positive result.

On July 20 the situation became desperate, and the pope was readmitted to Gemelli. A series of intricate clinical exams uncovered a new problem, cytomegalovirus, which the pope had contracted through the blood transfusions. The correct course of treatment began. On June 24 Karol Wojtyla's temperature returned to normal, and the pope was out of danger.

A mysterious coincidence occurred that very afternoon in a countryside in Herzegovina, an area that was part of communist Yugoslavia. A group of young people—two males and four females—returned home frightened, saying that they had seen a strange lady. Thus began Our Lady's apparitions at Medjugorje, a phenomenon that has attracted millions of people throughout the world.

The Church has not pronounced on the trustworthiness of the Medjugorje apparitions. However, theologians who looked into the matter have affirmed that the message of Our Lady there continues and completes the message the Virgin gave at Fatima. And these apparitions began on the very day the pope's health—compromised by a mysterious illness as a result of the attack on May 13, the anniversary of Our Lady's first appearance at Fatima—began to improve. That very day the doctors discovered the "enemy," a strange virus, and began to treat the pope effectively.

The coincidence gave rise to many stories. Supposed prophecies attributed to Sister Lucia and the appearances at Fatima began to circulate, but none were based on credible documentation. In Sister Lucia's *Memoirs*, however, there are allusions to other visions the three shepherd children received regarding a suffering pope:

> One day we spent our siesta down by my parents' well. Jacinta sat on the stone slabs on top of the well. Francisco and I climbed up a steep bank in search of wild honey among the brambles in a nearby thicket. After a little while, Jacinta called out to me, "Didn't you see the Holy Father?"
>
> "No."
>
> "I don't know how it was, but I saw the Holy Father in a very big house, kneeling by a table, with his head buried in his hands, and he was weeping. Outside the house there were many people.

Some of them were throwing stones, others were cursing him and using bad language. Poor Holy Father, we must pray very much for him…."

Another time we went to the cave called Lapa do Cabeço. As soon as we got there, we prostrated on the ground, saying the prayers the Angel had taught us. After some time, Jacinta stood up and called to me, "Can't you see all those highways and roads and fields full of people, who are crying with hunger and have nothing to eat? And the Holy Father in a church praying before the Immaculate Heart of Mary? And so many people praying with him?"

Some days later, she asked me, "Can I say that I saw the Holy Father and all those people?"

"No. Don't you see that that's part of the secret? If you do, they'll find out right away."

"All right! Then I'll say nothing at all!"[5]

It was thought that Jacinta's vision referred to Pius XII or Paul VI, pontiffs who suffered from accusations, insults and slanders during their time on Peter's throne. But looking at John Paul II's life leads people to conclude that he was the pope in the vision.

In December 1983, two and a half years after the attack, John Paul II went to the prison to meet the man who had tried to kill him. Alì Agca asked the pope why he wasn't dead because he knew he had taken proper aim. He was wondering what it was that people were saying about Fatima.

We do not know what the pope said. However, Alì Agca, in response to reporters' questions immediately after, said he felt the pope knew everything. Later, during the trial, Agca asked the Vatican to make the secret of Fatima public, indicating that he thought elements of it explained the attack.

CHAPTER SEVENTEEN

Pilgrimage to Fatima

WHILE HE WAS STAYING in the hospital, John Paul II began to plan a trip to Fatima to express his gratitude to Our Lady for the grace he had received. He set the date for May 13, 1982, one year after the attack.

During that trip his manner and the content of his speeches—as well as the passion, strength and distress with which he gave them—would make it clear that he had specific convictions about the attack on him and about the events of Fatima and the famous secret. He would give the distinct impression that he believed that the world was in grave danger and that he wanted to save it at all costs.

The pope arrived at Fatima on the evening of May 12, 1982, and spoke to the crowd gathered for the night vigil:

> I want to share something with you. For a long time I had been intending to come to Fatima, but when the attack at St. Peter's Square occurred a year ago, I immediately thought of this shrine and wanted to express my gratitude to Our Heavenly Mother for saving me from danger.... I saw in everything that happened—

and I'm not tired of repeating it—a special protection of Our
Lady. The coincidence about dates—and there are no mere coincidences in the design of Divine Providence—called our attention, and rather recalled it, to the message that was given here
through the three shepherd children, children of humble country
people, the little shepherds of Fatima, as they are universally
known…. And I am here, on behalf of the whole church, to hear
anew the message which went forth sixty-five years ago, proclaimed by the Mother who is concerned for the welfare of her
children.[1]

When he speaks in public, the pope weighs each word. His
manner of speaking indicated a "definite acknowledgment" of
the apparitions. It was a personal acknowledgment, of course,
but one coming from the pontiff, the head of the Church.

AFFIRMING THE MESSAGE

In 1930 the bishop of Leiria, after examining the events of
Fatima for a long time, had pronounced the apparitions "credible" and had allowed the veneration of Our Lady in that
place. Paul VI, in his 1967 trip to Fatima, had spoken of the
"veneration of Our Lady at Fatima." Karol Wotyla, for the first
time, emphasized the "certainty" that Our Lady was present in
these apparitions and that it was she who gave the message to
the three children.

That night the pope silently prayed for about forty minutes
before the statue of Our Lady at the site of the apparitions.
Then he took part in the evening procession with lit candles.
One million people from everywhere were with him. They
were exhausted, drenched by the rain, some barefoot with
bleeding feet. But they were full of faith, a kind of faith that, in
its simplicity and instinctive power, seems to create an umbil-
ical cord between creature and Creator.

The pope said that that he had come, as most of them had, with Mary's name on his lips and a heart full of praise for the mercy of God. Echoing Mary's prayer, the pope said that God had also done great things for him.

In 1967 on Paul VI's trip to Fatima, Sister Lucia had asked to be received by the pope, but Montini had told her to contact her bishop. The Church, while considering the apparitions authentic, held them at arm's length. They were considered "private revelation," which should not be of much interest to a pontiff. The Church actually was afraid of being discredited.

John Paul II, however, was not bound by that fear. On the morning of May 13 John Paul II went to meet Sister Lucia. He wanted to speak with her face-to-face, without witnesses or interpreters. He had the nun stand next to him for several photographs. Even this gesture was a sign of acknowledgment, of ascribing importance to Lucia and what she had said and written for years. He indicated that he understood its authentic value now after the attack.

During an open-air Mass the pope opened his heart to the enormous crowd, revealing the thoughts and concerns of his heart—and they were very serious thoughts and concerns. Speaking in an apocalyptic tone, in which he had never spoken before, he alluded to imminent dangers. He addressed Our Lady and prayed for her help with an almost desperate insistence. He expressed sorrow for the widespread abandonment of morality, the initial cause of a person's estrangement from the Creator. How can people not feel dismay, he wondered, over the spread of secularism and permissiveness noting how these undermine the essential values of Christian morality? The pope hoped his gesture would lead believers to seriously examine their commitment to the values of the gospel.

Wanting to identify himself with all the people and to present himself to God and to Our Lady simply as an individual—as a representative of the many who are confused and rebellious—he abandoned the normal orator's mode of expression. He did not analyze society or the world situation from his position as an observer, priest and pastor. Rather, he continued in the form of a prayer:

> The successor of Peter presents himself here also as a witness to the immensity of human suffering, a witness to the almost apocalyptic menaces looming over the nations and mankind as a whole.[2]

He used the exact words from Lucia's letters—"almost apocalyptic menaces"—and inferences from the content of the famous secret, which had been circulating for a while among groups of believers in Fatima but which were generally judged to be "fantastic," "exaggerated," "fanatical" and "without foundation." The pope now, in public and during a televised religious ceremony, was giving credence to those apocalyptic concerns.

THE CONSECRATION OF RUSSIA

For years Lucia had said that Our Lady wanted the Church to consecrate Russia to her Immaculate Heart. That consecration was a condition, a necessary step, for the conversion of Russia. She specified that the consecration needed to be made by the whole Church—that is, the pope in union with all the bishops. This was a very demanding request from a juridical and theological point of view in the sense that "the pope in union with all the bishops" needed to believe that the apparitions of Our Lady at Fatima and Lucia's subsequent revelations were authentic, or at least "worthy of great attention."

John Paul II on his 1982 trip took the request for the consecration of Russia into consideration. In a distressed tone he prayed to Our Lady for "the world of the second millennium that is drawing to a close, the modern world, our world today!" He then spoke the exact words for a consecration:

> Embrace, with the love of the Mother and Handmaid, this human world of ours, which we entrust and consecrate to you, for we are full of disquiet for the earthly and eternal destiny of individuals and peoples. In a special way we entrust and consecrate to you those individuals and nations which particularly need to be entrusted and consecrated.[3]

But who were those "individuals and nations which particularly need to be entrusted and consecrated"? The words certainly applied to the people under the communist regime. But why didn't the pope explicitly name Russia, as Our Lady had instructed Sister Lucia several times? Probably because he did not have the consent of the "whole Church," as he had not had time to consult the bishops. He had the intention of carrying out the consecration so often asked for upon his return to Rome. He was convinced it was necessary.

His heartfelt prayer continued:

> Help us to conquer the menace of evil, which so easily takes root in the hearts of the people of today, and whose immeasurable effects already weigh down upon our modern world and seem to block the paths towards the future![4]

John Paul II, optimistic and courageous by nature, would never have said such things if he did not have a clear vision of an imminent danger.

"From famine and war, *deliver us*," the pope prayed as he continued his intense supplication of the Virgin. "From nuclear war, from incalculable self-destruction, from every kind of war, *deliver us*."[5]

Here the phrase "from nuclear war" needs to be emphasized. This was the danger described at various times in the rumors about the secret and about Sister Lucia's interpretations.

These rumors were officially denied each time, but in the words spoken by the pope at Fatima that day, they seemed to find some resonance. He continued:

> From sins against the life of man from its very beginning, deliver us.... From every kind of injustice in the life of society, both national and international, deliver us.... From attempts to stifle in human hearts the very truth of God, deliver us.... Accept, O Mother of Christ, this cry laden with the sufferings of all individual human beings, laden with the sufferings of whole societies....[6] Today John Paul II, successor of Peter, continuer of the work of Pius, John, and Paul, and particular heir of the Second Vatican Council, presents himself before the Mother of the Son of God in her shrine at Fatima...reading again with trepidation the motherly call to penance, to conversion, the ardent appeal of the Heart of Mary that resounded at Fatima sixty-five years ago. Yes, he reads it again with trepidation in his heart, because he sees how many people and societies—how many Christians—have gone in the opposite direction to the one indicated in the message of Fatima. Sin has thus made itself firmly at home in the world, and denial of God has become widespread in the ideologies, ideas and plans of human beings.[7]

In 1982 we were still far from the fall of the Berlin Wall, from the fall of communism and even from a concrete and indisputable knowledge that the communist ideology had filled the world with its errors and had brought destruction to entire nations. We were also far from understanding that other atheistic ideologies would continue the destruction. It was necessary to help people understand, to seek the truth and to stop the descent to destruction.

John Paul II was not content with words and gestures. It is legitimate to assume that, on the day of that pilgrimage, he may have offered himself as a sacrifice for the salvation of humanity. And it is not fantastic to imagine that the suffering that followed may have been the price that he was willing to pay.

A papal souvenir remains at Fatima—the assassin's bullet, which the pope had given earlier to the bishop of Leiria-Fatima. It has been welded into the crown of the statue of Our Lady of Fatima.

This is a special crown weighing more than two and a half pounds. Decorated with 313 pearls and 2,676 precious stones, it was given to Our Lady by the women of Portugal. It is placed on the statue only on the twelfth and thirteenth day of every month and on other days is kept in a safe.

The dark, opaque, nine-millimeter bullet is now in the center of the crown and stands almost menacingly in contrast to the shining brilliance of the pearls and the precious stones. Its mysterious symbolism renders it undoubtedly the most precious jewel in the group. When the crown is placed on the statue's head, the bullet is less than an inch from Our Lady's head. But it is harmless, ineffective, powerless, just like the serpent that the Blessed Virgin crushed beneath her feet.

CHAPTER EIGHTEEN

Up the Mountain

JOHN PAUL II'S LIFE took on a new orientation as he understood that his mission was to journey "up a steep mountain, at the top of which there was a big Cross." At Fatima Our Lady spoke of prayer and penance; Wotyla decided to be a man of prayer and penance.

From that point on his life was a *Via Crucis*. Diseases, illnesses, hospitalizations and surgeries followed one after another. After he broke his shoulder in 1993, he confided to a friend that he saw this as one more opportunity to unite himself more intimately to the mystery of the Cross of Christ and to be in communion with so many suffering brothers and sisters. When he could barely stand up and could walk only with short steps, extremely fatigued, someone defined him as "a crucified one who walks."

But the sickness and difficulties did not stop his spiritual commitment on behalf of the world. Prayer became constant.

"In the end...Russia...will be converted," Our Lady said at Fatima in 1917.[1] John Paul II believed he should collaborate to see the fulfillment of that statement. He continued to ponder the famous request for the consecration of Russia to the Immaculate Heart of Mary.

MARY'S GOAL

There was a lot of talk about that consecration, and there still is. Some theologians, even those "favorable" to Fatima—those who believe that Our Lady can intervene in the destiny of the world through apparitions and messages—maintain that the request was absurd and unacceptable because it was presented as a condition for Russia's conversion. "It is impossible to believe," they say, "that God would make the conversion of a people conditional on a gesture, a ceremony and, on top of that, a certain kind of ceremony."

Our Lady first mentioned Russia's consecration on July 13, 1917, when she entrusted the secret to the three visionaries. She had shown the children hell and the souls who were falling into that sea of fire. She then asked "for the consecration of Russia to my Immaculate Heart, and the Communion of reparation on the First Saturdays."[2] Heeding this, she promised, would lead to Russia's conversion and peace; not heeding it would result in the spread of Russia's errors, wars and persecutions of the Church.

Both scholars and popularizers have stressed the Fatima message's prophetic tone in predicting wars, famines and ideologies that would spread errors throughout the world. One can deduce that the consecration of Russia and the Communion of reparations on the first Saturday of every month—requests also made at a later time—would have been able to avoid these evils. But they needed to be in place before 1939. Her requests were not heeded, and the evil she foresaw came to pass.

The two practices Our Lady requested—devotion to her Immaculate Heart and the Communion of reparation on first Saturdays—are simple, practical exercises that can remind believers of the fundamental truths of the faith and help them keep a balanced and vital connection to the spiritual realm. They are like the habit of sons and daughters who periodically visit their mothers or call them every Saturday evening.

All heavenly apparitions have this goal, and so do miracles, wonders and prophecies, of which the Church's history is replete with examples. They are helps or signs whose purpose is to highlight an aspect of the truth that has unfortunately become obscured. They can correct errors, strengthen ties and inspire fresh motivation for continuing on the path to the kingdom.

A RENEWED REQUEST

Our Lady asked Lucia to request the consecration of Russia in 1929. Sister Lucia writes in her *Memoirs*:

> At this time.... I had sought and obtained permission from my superiors and confessor to make a Holy Hour from eleven o'clock until midnight, every Thursday to Friday night. Being alone one night...the only light was that of the sanctuary lamp. Suddenly the whole chapel was illumined by a supernatural light, and above the altar appeared [many things: a cross, a dove, and so on]....
> Our Lady then said to me, "The moment has come in which God asks the Holy Father, in union with all the bishops of the world, to make the consecration of Russia to my Immaculate Heart, promising to save it by this means."
>
> I gave an account of this to the confessor.... Later in an intimate communication, Our Lord complained [that no one had paid attention to his request]: "They will repent and do it, but it will be late. Russia will have already spread her errors throughout the world, provoking wars, and persecutions of the Church; the Holy Father will have had much to suffer."[3]

JOHN PAUL II: A LIFE OF GRACE

Sister Lucia informed her confessor, who in turn informed the bishop of Leiria-Fatima, José da Silva Correia, because that was the proper procedure to follow. But it was a slow bureaucratic process. In fact, it was only in 1937 that the bishop of Leiria-Fatima wrote to Pius XI informing him of the request. Still nothing happened.

On December 2, 1940, Sister Lucia wrote to Pius XII, telling him the history of Our Lady's request. She added:

> In various intimate communications, the Lord has not ceased insisting on his request. He ultimately promises that if Your Holiness would consecrate the world to the Immaculate Heart of Mary with special mention of Russia—and do so with all the bishops of the world—he would shorten the days of tribulation with which the nations are being punished for their sins through war, famine, and persecution of the church and of Your Holiness.[4]

Pius XII believed in the apparitions at Fatima. He had been ordained a bishop on May 13, 1917, the exact day Our Lady first appeared at Fatima. When he learned of the Virgin's request, he immediately wanted to take some initiative. He did so in his radio message to Portugal for the twenty-fifth anniversary of the apparitions at Fatima on October 31, 1942. However, he could not see a way to mention Russia specifically. He repeated the consecration on December 8, 1942, the feast of the Immaculate Conception, but again without singling out Russia.

Finally, on July 17, 1952, the feast day of St. Cyril and St. Methodius, Pope Pius XII specifically consecrated Russia:

> Just as the whole world was consecrated to the Immaculate Heart of the Blessed Virgin, the Mother of God, a few years ago, so too today, in a special way, we consecrate all the people of Russia to her.[5]

But this was the pope's own initiative, not "in union with all the bishops," as Our Lady had requested.

Pope John XXIII certainly had a great devotion to Our Lady, but he did not consider the request of Fatima. Paul VI, on the other hand, consecrated the world on November 21, 1964, at the close of the third session of the Second Vatican Council, and repeated it on May 13, 1967, the fiftieth anniversary of the apparitions at Fatima. Both times he recalled the consecrations by Pius XII without highlighting Russia. John Paul I did not have time to consider the matter in his thirty-two days.

A VALID CONSECRATION

Bishop Paul Hnilica, a Czechoslovakian bishop who worked hard for the "Church of Silence" in countries under the communist regime and was a friend of Wojtyla from when he became a cardinal in Kraków, told me:

> When the pope was elected, I told John Paul II, "I'm happy about your election. I am sure that God has chosen you because you need to consecrate Russia to the Immaculate Heart of Mary. If that doesn't happen, your pontificate will be incomplete." He answered, "I am ready to do it if you can convince the bishops to join me."
>
> I returned to the topic when I went to visit him at Gemelli Hospital after the attack: "Our Lady was referring to you when she said at Fatima, 'The Holy Father will have much to suffer.'" "All the pontiffs have to suffer much for the church," he responded.
>
> I reminded him of Jacinta's vision. The little shepherdess had seen the Holy Father struck down with his white robe stained with blood, and he said, "Yes, that detail about the blood could refer to the attack."
>
> Karol Wojtyla was hospitalized for more than two months and suffered severely. New complications and new infections kept coming up. He wanted to die. He said that in his condition he would not be of much use to the church, so he was praying that the Lord would take him to heaven. But he always added, "May God's will be done."

When he finally left the hospital, I gave him a statuette of Our Lady of Fatima. He blessed it and kissed it, saying, "In these months of suffering and struggle between life and death, I have come to understand that the only solution to the dire problems in today's world is prayer. Humanity must be saved from deadly wars and the militant atheism which is still spreading in order for Russia to be converted, as Our Lady said." I again reminded him of the consecration requested by the Blessed Virgin as the means of attaining that conversion.

Shortly after, on December 8, 1981, the pope celebrated mass at St. Mary Major. He prayed for all the Eastern European countries, entrusting these countries to Our Lady. In the sacristy I said to him, "Holy Father, the messages of Our Lady of Fatima ask for the consecration of Russia, which is not the same as entrusting it." "I know," he answered, "but many theologians oppose using the word 'consecration.'"

On May 13, 1982, when the pope made a pilgrimage to Fatima, I was also present. At noon the bishop of Fatima announced that at 7:00 p.m. the pope would pray at the site of the apparitions and that any bishops and cardinals present could join him if they wished.

Everyone was present at 7:00. I was next to Cardinal Franciszek Macharski, the Archbishop of Kraków. The pope was very focused when he arrived and greeted no one. He passed by without noticing me, but after he took a few steps, he turned back and said to me in Polish, "Today you will be the most contented, happiest, and most satisfied bishop present." As soon as he left, everyone gathered around to ask me what he had said. I didn't want to translate so Cardinal Macharski did, but it didn't come through accurately: "We will all be happy." Even I did not quite understand his meaning at first, but looking at the Polish text of the prayer the pope was going to say, I understood. He was going to "consecrate" Russia in that prayer. But he was doing that on his own. It was not with all the bishops as Our Lady had asked.

Returning to Rome, the pope devoted himself to fulfilling the Blessed Virgin's request. He wrote to all the bishops and, on March 25, 1984, in Rome, John Paul II, spiritually united to all the bishops, finally made the consecration of the world and of Russia to Our Lady.

> Was it a valid consecration? It is hard to say. Several days later, the pope, speaking of what he had done, asked me, "How many bishops were really united with me? That's the problem." I asked Sister Lucia later what she thought and she said, "The Holy Father did everything he could, so Jesus is content. However, not all the bishops are united with him. The consecration is valid but has not reached its fullness."

Our Lady's request encountered great obstacles. The fact remains that near the end of the twentieth century, unimaginable things occurred: the fall of the Berlin Wall, Gorbachev's visit to the Vatican and the fall of the communist regime in Eastern Europe. These events completely altered the world's landscape.

"DO NOT BE AFRAID!"

On May 13, 1991, ten years after the attack, John Paul II returned to Fatima. During his speeches on this trip, there was no apocalyptic tone. He denounced some serious situations and the abandonment of morality, and he encouraged necessary changes. But his words were full of serenity and great hope:

> Faced with the devastation which is shaking diverse continents here and there and with the fast pace of the upheaval of values which lays snares against moral certitude and even the life of nations, I make the hope of St. Augustine my own. In the midst of an assault by vandals on the city of Hippo, a concerned group of Christians from his church came to him. He said, "Do not be afraid, dear sons. This is not the end of the old world so much as it is the beginning of a new world." A new dawn seems to be on the horizon for history, inviting Christians to be salt and light in a world that has an enormous need for Christ, the redeemer of all of humanity.[6]

Has the apocalyptic danger for humanity passed? We do not know, but one thing is certain: Due to the mystical impact of

John Paul II and of the millions of people who are spiritually united to him and have prayed and suffered with him, the world has surely begun to change. The pope said at the conclusion of his trip:

> There seems to be a consoling light overflowing with hope spreading from Fatima that is shedding light on events at the end of the second millennium. The events that marked 1989 and the initial months of 1990 have caused a crucial turning point in history for this difficult twentieth century. A new perspective is now opening up for the journey of the nations.[7]

These are words of hope—great hope—although events in various nations of the world have continued on a chaotic course. John Paul II is always present, always ready to comfort, to encourage, to explain, to support, to show the way and to carry forth the truth of Christ. Above all, he is always ready to carry in his own body the mystery of suffering and of the cross with its redeeming power.

The pope is becoming more "conformed" to the "Bishop dressed in white" who, "half trembling with halting step afflicted with pain and sorrows," climbs up a steep mountain. John Paul II is climbing up toward the cross, without ceasing to speak to the world. His voice, sometimes so weak as to be imperceptible, continues to proclaim hope and to point to the secret that saves: "Do not be afraid to open the door to Christ!"

He uttered this cry during his first speech as pope in October 1978, and he has often repeated it throughout the course of his ministry. He repeated it again in 2003, during the homily of his anniversary Mass in St. Peter's Square:

> From the beginning of my Pontificate, my thoughts, prayers and actions were motivated by one desire: to witness that Christ, the Good Shepherd, is present and active in his Church. He is constantly searching for every stray sheep, to lead it back to the

sheepfold, to bind up its wounds; he tends the sheep that are weak and sickly and protects those that are strong. This is why, from the very first day, I have never ceased to urge people: "Do not be afraid to welcome Christ and accept his power!"…

Today I forcefully repeat: "Open, indeed, open wide the doors to Christ!" Let him guide you! Trust in his love![8]

Notes

INTRODUCTION
A Record-Setting Pope

1. Televised ceremony, October 18, 1978.
2. *Ibid.*
3. *Ibid.*

CHAPTER ONE
The Bishop Dressed in White

1. Sister Lucia, *Fatima in Lucia's Own Words*, ed. by Fr. Louis Kondor, trans. by Dominican Nuns of Perpetual Rosary (Cambridge, Mass.: Ravengate Press, 1976). The material in this chapter describing the events of July 13, 1917, is taken from pages 108-109, 165, 169.
2. *Ibid.*
3. *Ibid.*
4. www.vatican.va. Address of Cardinal Angelo Sodano, May 13, 2000.
5. www.vatican.va. Third part of the secret.
6. www.vatican.va. Address of Cardinal Sodano, May 13, 2000.
7. www.vatican.va. Theological commentary of Cardinal Joseph Ratzinger, prefect of the Congregation for the Doctrine of the Faith on June 26, 2000.

CHAPTER TWO
Origins

1. Luciano Bergonzoni, *Emilia Kaczorowska in Wojtyla: La mamma di Giovanni Paolo II* (Vigodarzere: Edizioni Carroccio, 1998).
2. *Ibid.*
3. Pope John Paul II, *Gift and Mystery* (New York: Doubleday, 1996), p. 20.
4. André Frossard, *"Be Not Afraid!"*, trans. by J. R. Foster (New York: St. Martin's Press, 1984), p. 14.
5. Pope John Paul II. *The Place Within: The Poetry of Pope John Paul II,* trans. by Jerzy Peterkiewicz (New York: Random House, 1982), p. ix.

CHAPTER THREE
The Captain's School

1. Pope John Paul II, *Pilgrim to Poland,* compiled by the Daughters of St. Paul (Boston: Pauline Books & Media, 1979), p. 197.
2. Frossard, p. 14.
3. Pope John Paul II, *Gift and Mystery*, p. 20.
4. Bergonzoni, *Emilia Kaczorowska in Wojtyla.*
5. Frossard, p. 14.

CHAPTER FOUR
Edmund's Sacrifice

1. Bergonzoni, *Emilia Kaczorowska in Wojtyla,* p. 68.
2. Luciano Bergonzoni, *Edmondo Wojtyla: Medico polacco vittima del dovere* (Padova: Centro Editoriale Carroccio, 1992), p. 67.
3. *Ibid.,* p. 63.
4. Frossard, p. 14.
5. Bergonzoni, *Edmondo Wojtyla,* p. 41.

CHAPTER FIVE
"The Ballad of Spring"

1. Pope John Paul II, *Gift and Mystery,* pp. 5-6.
2. Carl Bernstein and Marco Politi, *His Holiness: John Paul II and the Hidden History of Our Time* (New York: Doubleday, 1996), p. 45.

CHAPTER SIX
Entering the Arena

1. Pope John Paul II, *Gift and Mystery,* pp. 7-8.
2. James Michener, *Poland* (New York: Fawcett-Crest, 1983), p. 451.

CHAPTER SEVEN
The Tailor's School

1. Pope John Paul II, *Gift and Mystery,* pp. 27-28.
2. *Ibid.,* p. 23.
3. *Ibid.,* p. 24.
4. *Ibid.,* pp. 29-30.
5. Frossard, p. 18.

CHAPTER EIGHT
New Pursuits

1. Bernstein and Politi, p. 62.
2. Pope John Paul II, *Gift and Mystery,* p. 34.
3. *Ibid.*, pp. 34-36.

CHAPTER NINE
Training for the Priesthood

1. Pope John Paul II, *Gift and Mystery*, p. 3.
2. Bernstein and Politi, p. 57.
3. *Ibid.*, p. 69.

CHAPTER TEN
The Young Priest

1. Bernstein and Politi, p. 70.

CHAPTER ELEVEN
Confronting Communism

1. George Weigel, *Witness to Hope* (New York: HarperCollins, 1999), pp. 97-98.
2. Karol Wojtyla (Pope John Paul II), *Love and Responsibility*, trans. by H. T. Willets (New York: William Collins Sons & Co., 1981), p. 221.
3. *Ibid.*, p. 276.
4. *Ibid.*, p. 273.

CHAPTER TWELVE
This is My Path

1. Bernstein and Politi. The account of Wyszyński's meeting with Wojtyla can be found on pp. 87-88.

CHAPTER THIRTEEN
A Staunch Bishop

1. Bernstein and Polliti, pp. 110-111.

CHAPTER FOURTEEN
New Power in Kraków

1. Mieczyslaw Maliński, *Pope John Paul II: The Life of Karol Wojtyla* (New York: Seabury Press, 1979), pp. 198-199.
2. Weigel, p. 190.

CHAPTER FIFTEEN
A Pope from a Distant Country

1. Andrea Torniella and Alessandro Zangrando, *Papa Luciani, il parroco del mondo* (Udine: Edizione Sengo, 1998), p. 182.

CHAPTER SIXTEEN
One Hand Shoots, Another Hand Saves

1. Frossard, p. 251.
2. www. vatican.va. From third part of the secret, original text.
3. www.vatican.va.
4. Bernstein and Politi, p. 297.
5. Sister Lucia, *Fatima in Lucia's Own Words*, pp. 112-113.

CHAPTER SEVENTEEN
Pilgrimage to Fatima

1. Domenico Del Rio, *Wojtyla, un pontificato itinerate* (Bologna: Edizioni Dehoniane, 1994), p. 225.
2. *L'Osservatore Romano*, English Edition, "Message of Mary's Maternal Love," May 17, 1982.
3. *L'Osservatore Romano*, English Edition, "Act of Consecration," May 24, 1982.
4. *Ibid.*
5. *Ibid.*
6. *Ibid.*
7. *L'Osservatore Romano*, English Edition, "Message of Mary's Maternal Love," May 17, 1982.

CHAPTER EIGHTEEN
Up the Mountain

1. Sister Lucia, *Fatima in Lucia's Own Words,* p. 109.
2. *Ibid.*, p. 109.
3. *Ibid.*, pp. 198-199.
4. Umberto M. Pasquale, *Fatima e Blasar, Celeste Gemellaggio* (Milan: Lampade Viventi, 1975), p. 30.
5. *Papal Documents on Mary (*Milwaukee: The Bruce Publishing Company, 1954), pp. 249-251, as quoted on www.ewtn.com.
6. Del Rio, p. 694.
7. *Ibid.*, p. 700.
8. *L'Osservatore Romano*, "Homily at the Mass Inaugurating the Pontifical Ministry of John Paul II," English edition, November 2, 1978, p. 12.